BASICS *of*
HEBREW
ACCENTS

BASICS *of*

HEBREW

ACCENTS

Mark D. Futato, Sr.

ZONDERVAN ACADEMIC

Basics of Hebrew Accents
Copyright © 2020 by Mark D. Futato

Requests for information should be addressed to:
Zondervan, *3900 Sparks Dr. SE, Grand Rapids, Michigan 49546*

ISBN 978-0-310-09842-3 (softcover)

Cover photo: Zondervan

Printed in the United States of America

HB 03.19.2024

To Adele,
who has been with me
since I first learned the difference between aleph and bet.

CONTENTS

ABBREVIATIONS

AFPMA	*Andersen Forbes Phrase Marker Analysis.* Andersen, Francis I., and A. Dean Forbes. Bellingham, WA: Lexham Press, n.d.
BHRG	*A Biblical Hebrew Reference Grammar.* Van der Merwe, Christo H. J., Jacobus A. Naudé, and Kroeze, Jan H. 2nd ed. London: T&T Clark, 2017
DCH	*Dictionary of Classical Hebrew.* Edited by David J. A. Clines. 9 vols. Sheffield: Sheffield Phoenix Press, 1993–2014
ESV	English Standard Version
GKC	*Gesenius' Hebrew Grammar.* Edited by Emil Kautzsch. Translated by Arthur E. Cowley. 2nd ed. Oxford: Clarendon, 1910
HALOT	*The Hebrew and Aramaic Lexicon of the Old Testament.* Ludwig Koehler, Walter Baumgartner, and Johann J. Stamm. Translated and edited under the supervision of Mervyn E. J. Richardson. 4 vols. Leiden: Brill, 1994–1999
Joüon	Joüon, Paul. *A Grammar of Biblical Hebrew.* Translated and revised by T. Muraoka. 2 vols. 2nd ed. Rome: Gregorian University Press, 2011
NASB	New American Standard Bible
NIV	New International Version
NLT	New Living Translation
NRSV	New Revised Standard Version
NJPS	*Tanakh: The Holy Scriptures: The New JPS Translation according to the Traditional Hebrew Text*
WO	Waltke, Bruce K., and M. O'Connor. *An Introduction to Biblical Hebrew Syntax.* Winona Lake, IN: Eisenbrauns, 1990

INTRODUCTION

Perhaps you have just finished an introduction to Hebrew grammar, and you are excited to begin reading the biblical texts. You open the Hebrew Bible to Genesis 1:1, and your first reaction is to question the seemingly odd marks on the Hebrew words and wonder how you have forgotten so much so quickly. What you have noticed, perhaps for the first time, are the Hebrew accents.

When I began my study of Hebrew grammar in the mid-seventies, I used what was the standard teaching grammar for many years, *Introduction to Biblical Hebrew* by Thomas Lambdin.[1] Lambdin's introductory grammar did not contain any information on the Hebrew accents, and the same is true for most introductory grammars today.[2] It is a rare student who has been introduced to the Hebrew accents through an introductory grammar. For that matter, most students who have taken advanced classes in Hebrew are confused when they first meet the accents because they too have not studied them.

In this book I will not only introduce you to the accents, but you will learn how to use them to be a better reader of the Hebrew Bible.

Let's be clear up front: The accents are complicated and can be perplexing. One scholar said, "This system is exceedingly obscure, it is indeed one of signs and wonders."[3] But you do not need to know every detail of the

---

1. Thomas O. Lambdin, *Introduction to Biblical Hebrew* (London: Darton, Longman & Todd, 1973).

2. A couple of exceptions are (1) Duane A. Garrett and Jason S. DeRouchie, *A Modern Grammar for Biblical Hebrew* (Nashville: Broadman & Holman, 2009), which contains six pages (273–78); (2) Arthur Walker-Jones, *Hebrew for Biblical Interpretation* (Atlanta: SBL Press, 2003), which contains two and a half pages (69–72); and (3) Gary D. Pratico and Miles V. Van Pelt, *Basics of Biblical Hebrew Grammar*, 3rd ed. (Grand Rapids: Zondervan, 2019), which contains three paragraphs (405–6). My own grammar—Mark D. Futato, *Beginning Biblical Hebrew* (Winona Lake, IN: Eisenbrauns, 2003)—contains no information on the accents.

3. Arthur Davis, *The Hebrew Accents of the Twenty-One Books of the Bible* (Leopold Classic Library, 1900; repr., London: Myers & Co.), 12.

Hebrew accents to have a working knowledge that will help you in reading and interpreting the text. When you first learned Hebrew, you did not study a detailed reference grammar like *A Grammar of Biblical Hebrew*[4] or *A Biblical Hebrew Reference Grammar*,[5] which contain far more information than any introductory grammar. Had you started with such a grammar, you would have gotten lost in the forest for the trees. Like an introduction to the basics of Hebrew grammar, this book is an introduction to the basics of Hebrew accents. Every minute detail will not be covered, but you will learn enough about the accents to eliminate perplexity and make interpretive friends of the accents. Once you have mastered this basic material, you will be equipped to move on to study the accents in greater detail.[6]

There are two related but different sets of accents in the Hebrew Bible. One set is used for the Twenty-One while the other set is used for the Three. The Three include Psalms, the poetry of Job, and Proverbs. The Twenty-One include the rest of the books of the Hebrew Bible. Most of this book will discuss the accents in the Twenty-One (chs. 1–4), while an overview will be provided for the accents in the Three (ch. 5).

In chapter 1 the three basic jobs of the Hebrew accents will be introduced. The accents are indicators of (1) the stressed syllable in words—word stress, (2) the syntactic relationship between words—sense, and (3) the intonation of words for singing—chanting. The first and third of these jobs can be covered relatively quickly, so we will include a discussion of them in chapter 1. The second job is the one that is most helpful for reading your Hebrew Bible, and it will be our focus in the rest of the book.

Chapter 2 will cover the disjunctive accents. By the end of this chapter you will know the names, symbols, and functions of these accents. Chapter 3 will cover the conjunctive accents—their names, symbols, and functions. By the end of chapters 2 and 3 you will know the difference between, for example, *munakh* (בְּרָא) and *atnakh* (אֱלֹהִים) and the roles they play in the interpretation of the text.

---

4. Paul Joüon and T. Muraoka, *A Grammar of Biblical Hebrew*, 2nd ed. (Rome: Gregorian University Press, 2011).

5. Christo H. J. van der Merwe, J. A. Naudé, and J. H. Kroeze, *A Biblical Hebrew Reference Grammar*, 2nd ed. (London: T&T Clark, 2017).

6. See Appendix 2 for further study.

In chapter 4 we will put our knowledge of the accents to work by reading particular verses through the lens of the accents. Paying attention to the accents will at times make a subtle difference in our interpretation of the text. At other times the difference will be much more significant. Then we will take a look at a couple of examples where it seems to be the case that the masoretic accents are incorrect. By the end of chapter 4 you will have a solid foundation of the basics of the Hebrew accents.

Chapter 5 will introduce you to the accents in the Three, including a brief study of the accents in Psalm 29. There are two appendices at the end of the book, one will provide a preliminary guide for showing you why the accents occur as they do, and the other will provide material for further study.

One article says,

> The Masoretic pointing as a whole, and the punctuation in particular, is arguably one of the greatest literary and linguistic achievements in history. Its development spanned more than a thousand years and was only possible through the co-operation of countless forgotten scholars whose dedication to accuracy was without parallel. It offers to all the "people of the Book" a detailed explanation of how the great biblical teachers understood their sacred text.[7]

What a privilege we have of getting to know "one of the greatest literary and linguistic achievements in history." While I can't deny that the accent system is complicated, I can promise you that a basic knowledge of the Hebrew accents will make you a better reader of your Hebrew Bible.

Your Hebrew Bible begins with בְּרֵאשִׁית ("In the beginning"). That odd mark under the *shin* might confuse you at the moment, but soon you will know that its name is *tiphkha* and that it wants you to pause just a bit before going on. So, pause for a moment, take a deep breath, then jump into chapter 1 to learn more about the three basic jobs of the Hebrew accents.

---

7. David Robinson and Elisabeth Levy, "The Masoretes and the Punctuation of Biblical Hebrew," *British & Foreign Bible Society* (May 2, 2002): 25, http://lc.bfbs.org.uk/e107_files/downloads/masoretes.pdf.

THE THREE JOBS OF THE ACCENTS

Each accent carries out three related jobs. Every time an accent is used, it carries out all three jobs at the same time. Before we look at these three jobs, let's meet the accents, at least briefly, in terms of their names in Hebrew and English and their symbols.[1] The first chart lists the names and symbols of the disjunctive accents, and the second chart does the same for the conjunctive accents. (By the end of the chapter, you will know the difference between these two kinds of accents.) The accents in the first chart are batched into four groups. In chapter 2 you will learn the significance of these groups for interpreting your Hebrew Bible. For now, learning this first list of accents by group (or in smaller chunks) will make the memorization of the English names and the symbols easier. Memorize the English names now along with their corresponding symbols, as this will make it much easier for you to absorb the material that follows in the remainder of the book. The far-right column shows you what each symbol looks like, and the column to the left shows where you can expect to find each symbol on a Hebrew word. (As you have probably already learned, the accents fall on the last syllable of a word most of the time.)

---

1. The font used in this book (SBL Hebrew Font) differs somewhat from the font used in BHS. In general, the BHS font has straight lines where the SBL font has curves (compare *tiphkha* on בְּרֵאשִׁית in Gen 1:1). One particular is that in BHS *zarqa* looks like a question mark without the dot and slanted to the right, where the SBL font has backward "s" lying on its side (compare *zarqa* on אֱלֹהִים֮ in Gen 1:7). The font used in this book will match up with the fonts in Bible study software like Logos and Accordance.

Disjunctive Accents

Group	Hebrew Name	English Name	Symbol	Symbol
Group 1	סִלּוּק	silluq	טטט	֯
	אַתְנָח	atnakh	טטט	֑
Group 2	סְגוֹלְתָּא	segolta	טטט	֒
	שַׁלְשֶׁלֶת	shalshelet	טטט|	|֓
	זָקֵף קָטוֹן	zaqeph qaton	טטט	֔
	זָקֵף גָּדוֹל	zaqeph gadol	טטט	֕
	טִפְחָה	tiphkha	טטט	֖
Group 3	רְבִיעַ	revia	טטט	֗
	זַרְקָא	zarqa	טטט	֮
	פַּשְׁטָא	pashta	טטט	֙
	תְּבִיר	tevir	טטט	֛
	יְתִיב	yetiv	טטט	֚
Group 4	פָּזֵר	pazer	טטט	֡
	קַרְנֵי פָרָה[2]	qarne parah[2]	טטט	֟
	תְּלִישָׁא גְדוֹלָה	telisha gedolah	טטט	֠
	גֶּרֶשׁ	geresh	טטט	֜
	גֵּרְשַׁיִם	gershayim	טטט	֞
	לְגַרְמֵהּ	legarmeh	טטט|	|֣

---

2. An alternative name is *pazer gadol* (פָּזֵר גָּדוֹל). I prefer *qarne parah* because it means "horns of a cow," which is what the symbol looks like, so it should be easier to remember.

Conjunctive Accents

Hebrew Name	English Name	Symbol	Symbol
מֵרְכָא	merekha	טטט	֭
מֵרְכָא כְּפוּלָה	merekha kephulah	טטט	֞
מוּנַח	munakh	טטט	֣
מְהֻפָּח	mehuppakh	טטט	֤
דַּרְגָּא	darga	טטט	֧
אַזְלָא	azla[3]	טטֹט	֢
תְּלִישָׁא קְטַנָּה	telisha qetannah	טטֹט	֩
גַּלְגַּל	galgal	טטט	֪

Don't let these lists intimidate you. While there are twenty-six accents listed, you will be focusing on a little more than one-half of them. By the end of this book, those that you focus on will be as familiar to you as the consonants and vowels that make up their Hebrew names.

JOB #1: WORD STRESS

When you first began reading Biblical Hebrew, you probably struggled with remembering where to accent a word. You learned that, in general, Hebrew places the stress on the last syllable—but not always. Your instructor may have assured you, as I assure my students, that once you open your Hebrew Bible, this problem will disappear, because every word will have an accent that shows you where the stress lies—but not always!

We called the above listed symbols "accents" because most of the time they indicate the stressed syllable. We can call the following accents impositive,[4] as opposed to prepositive or postpositive, terms which will be

---

3. An alternative name is *qadma* (קַדְמָא).
4. So Israel Yeivin, *Introduction to the Tiberian Masorah*, trans. and ed. E. J. Revell, The Society of Biblical Literature Masoretic Studies 5 (Missoula, MT: Scholars Press, 1980), 176.

addressed below. Impositive simply means "on the stressed syllable." Let's look at some examples.

Silluq ⟨◌⟩ *Silluq* is a small vertical stroke placed underneath the stressed syllable, as in the word הָאָֽרֶץ (Gen 1:1). When you learned the word אֶרֶץ, you learned to place the stress on the next to the last syllable, and the Hebrew accent confirms this.

Atnakh ⟨◌⟩ *Atnakh* looks like a small upside-down tuning fork or caret placed underneath the stressed syllable, as in the word אֱלֹהִים (Gen 1:1). By now you are accustomed to pronouncing אֱלֹהִים with the stress on the final syllable.

Zaqeph ⟨◌⟩ *Zaqeph*[5] looks like a small colon placed above the stressed syllable, as in the word אֱלֹהִים (Gen 1:2).

Tiphkha ⟨◌⟩ *Tiphkha* looks like a small, angled, left parenthesis placed below the stressed syllable, as in the word בְּרֵאשִׁית (Gen 1:1).

Revia ⟨◌⟩ *Revia* looks like a small square turned on its edge or diamond placed above the stressed syllable, as in the word וְהָאָרֶץ (Gen 1:2).

Geresh ⟨◌⟩ *Geresh* looks like a small angled left parenthesis placed above the stressed syllable, as in the word הַמַּיִם (Gen 1:9).

Merekha ⟨◌⟩ *Merekha* looks like a small, angled, right parenthesis placed below the stressed syllable, as in the word וַיֹּאמֶר (Gen 1:3).

Munakh ⟨◌⟩ *Munakh* looks like a small backward L placed below the stressed syllable, as in the word בָּרָא (Gen 1:1).

Mehuppakh ⟨◌⟩ *Mehuppakh* looks like a small less than sign placed below the stressed syllable, as in the word נֶפֶשׁ (Gen 1:24).

---

5. In this book I will use *zaqeph* as shorthand for *zaqeph qaton*. *Zaqeph gadol* is a substitute for *zaqeph qaton*, and *zaqeph qaton* occurs over 25,000 times whereas *zaqeph gadol* occurs only a bit over 1,600 times. When context demands, I will differentiate with the use of *qaton* and *gadol*.

Sometimes the Hebrew accent is not placed on the stressed syllable. There are two kinds of accents in this regard: prepositive and postpositive. Prepositive accents are placed at the very front of a word, regardless of where the stress lies. Let's look at some examples.

Yetiv ֚ *Yetiv* looks like a small less-than sign placed below and to the right of the first letter in a word, as in the word עֵ֚שֶׂב (Gen 1:11). [*Yetiv* and *mehuppakh* look alike, but they can always be distinguished based on the position of the accent. *Yetiv* will always be placed to the right of the vowel, whereas *mehuppakh* will be placed to the left; compare כִּ֚ (*yetiv* in Gen 3:5) and כִּ֤ (*mehuppakh* in Gen 4:12).][6]

Telisha Gedolah ֠ *Telisha gedolah* looks like a small angled-to-the-right lollipop placed above and to the right of the first letter in a word, as in the word הָ֠אָרֶץ (Gen 1:30). Note that the word הָ֠אָרֶץ is stressed on the second syllable from the end, not on the first syllable, where the accent is found.[7]

Postpositive accents are placed at the very end of a word, regardless of where the stress lies. Let's look at some examples.

Segolta ֒ *Segolta* looks like an upside-down *segol* placed above and to the left of the last letter in a word, as in the word הָרָקִ֒יעַ (Gen 1:7). The stress falls on קִי.[8]

Pashta ֙ *Pashta* looks like a small, angled, right parenthesis placed above and to the left of the last letter in a word, as in the word לָא֙וֹר (Gen 1:5). If the stressed syllable is not

---

6. *Yetiv* was made prepositive in order to distinguish it from *mehuppakh*; see William Wickes, *A Treatise on the Accentuation of the Twenty-One So-Called Prose Books of the Old Testament: With a Facsimile of a Page of the Codex Assigned to Ben-Asher in Aleppo* (Leopold Classic Library, 1887; repr., Oxford: Clarendon), 20.

7. *Telisha gedolah* was made prepositive to distinguish it from the circule, which indicates a masoretic note in the margin of the text; see Wickes, *A Treatise on the Twenty-One*, 22.

8. *Segolta* was made prepositive to keep from blending with *holem*; see Wickes, *A Treatise on the Twenty-One*, 17.

the final syllable, *pashta* will be repeated on the stressed syllable, as in the word הַמַּיִם (Gen 1:7), where the stress falls on מַּ.

Telisha ̊ ̊   *Telisha qetannah* looks like a small angled-to-the-left
Qetannah   lollipop placed above and to the left of the last letter in a word, as in the word אֱלֹהִים (Gen 1:25), where the stress falls on הִים.[9]

So, we call the above listed symbols "accents" because most of the time they indicate the stressed syllable in a word. But they have another job, and with that job comes another name for the symbols.

JOB #2: SENSE

The second job of the accents is to provide insight into the sense of the text.[10]

> The accent system punctuates the text and is therefore a very important feature in its syntactic analysis; despite the term accent, the system does not primarily refer to the pitch or duration of the words. This feature of Hebrew grammar is so important for understanding that medieval Jewish sources paid more attention to it than to establishing the correct pronunciation of words.[11]

One Hebrew label for the accents is טְעָמִים, the plural of the singular word טַעַם, which means "sense." While it seems a bit awkward, we could also call the accents "senses" or perhaps "sense markers" to reflect this ancient Hebrew nomenclature.

---

9. *Telisha qetannah* was made postpositive to distinguish it from the circule, which indicates a masoretic note in the margin of the text; see Wickes, *A Treatise on the Twenty-One*, 22.

10. "The Masoretes, the custodians and guardians of the Hebrew text of the Old Testament, inherited and handed down the traditional vocalizing and chanting of the text. This often indicates the traditional syntax and exegesis of the text." Russell T. Fuller and Kyoungwon Choi, *Invitation to Biblical Hebrew Syntax: An Intermediate Grammar* (Grand Rapids: Kregel Academic, 2017), 351.

11. WO §1.6.4.a.

This second job is not unrelated to the first job. For example, שָׁבוּ (from שׁוּב; Josh 2:22) means "returned" but שָׁבְוּ (from שׁבה; 1 Kgs 8:48) means "carried captive."[12] In such cases, where the stress falls on a word is significant for the sense of the word. At this point, however, our interest is more in the fact that the accents as sense markers provide us with an ancient commentary on what we nowadays call the syntax of the text.[13] While the sense markers as we know them go back to around CE 1000, there is evidence that the oral system that they encode goes back to around 200 BCE.[14] And even though these sense markers are not above criticism, we can think of them "as an early and relatively reliable witness to a correct interpretation of the text."[15]

The next two chapters are devoted to the details of the sense markers. For now, let's get the big picture. There are two kinds of sense markers. Some batch words together into syntactic units, while others separate one unit from another. The former we call "conjunctive" and the latter we call "disjunctive."

Disjunctive Accents

The disjunctive sense markers indicate where the reader is to pause in the reading of the text. The strength of these pauses varies with the symbol, somewhat like pauses in English punctuation: a period is a stronger pause than a semicolon, and a semicolon is a stronger pause than a comma. The pauses mark the end of a unit of one length or another. Let's look at a couple of examples of disjunctive accents.

---

12. Yeivin, *Introduction to the Tiberian Masorah*, 158.

13. James D. Price (*Concordance of the Hebrew Accents in the Hebrew Bible*, 5 vols. [Lewiston, NY: Mellen, 1996], 1.19–20) says, "It is true that the placement of the disjunctive accents usually coincides with the places where syntactic divisions occur in the Hebrew language of the text." Price explains the disharmony that sometimes occurs between the disjunctive accents and the syntax of the Hebrew text in terms of the musical function of the accents. Marcus A. Lehman (*Reading with the Masoretes: The Exegetical Utility of Masoretic Accent Patterns* [Wilmore, KY: GlossaHouse, 2019], 32) acknowledges the syntactic role of the accents and argues that at times accents are placed for semantic rather than syntactic reasons.

14. WO §1.6.4.a.

15. WO §1.6.4.b.

Example #1: Genesis 1:3

וַיֹּאמֶר אֱלֹהִים יְהִי אֹור וַיְהִי־אֹור:

Atnakh (אֹור) has the reader pause after reading what God said (יְהִי אֹור, "Let there be light") before reading what happened as a result of God speaking (וַיְהִי־אֹור, "and there was light"). *Tiphkha* (אֱלֹהִים) has the reader pause to a lesser degree after reading the introduction to God's speech (וַיֹּאמֶר אֱלֹהִים, "And God said") before reading what God actually said (יְהִי אֹור, "Let there be light").

Example #2: Genesis 1:10

וַיִּקְרָא אֱלֹהִים׀ לַיַּבָּשָׁה אֶרֶץ
וּלְמִקְוֵה הַמַּיִם קָרָא יַמִּים
וַיַּרְא אֱלֹהִים כִּי־טֹוב:

Atnakh (יַמִּים) has the reader pause after reading God's action of naming ("God called the dry ground 'land,' and the gathered waters he called 'seas.'") before reading God's action of evaluating ("And God saw that it was good."). *Zaqeph* (אֶרֶץ) has the reader pause to a lesser degree after reading God's naming the land ("God called the dry ground 'land'") before reading God's naming the gathered water ("and the gathered waters he called 'seas.'").

Conjunctive Accents

The conjunctive sense markers, on the other hand, require the reader to keep going and to read a word closely with what follows. Let's look at a couple of examples of conjunctive accents.

Example #1: Genesis 1:2b[16]

וְרוּחַ אֱלֹהִים מְרַחֶפֶת עַל־פְּנֵי הַמָּיִם:

---

16. An "a" or a "b" as part of a Bible reference indicates everything from the beginning of the verse up to and including *atnakh* and everything following *atnakh* to the end of the verse, respectively. So, 1:2b indicates the second half of verse 2.

Conjunctives are often found on the first of two words in a construct relationship. *Munakh* (וְר֫וּחַ, "and the spirit of") marks the noun in construction with אֱלֹהִ֑ים ("God"). And *merekha* (עַל־פְּנֵ֣י, "over the surface of" [NLT]) marks the phrase in construction with הַמָּ֑יִם ("the waters").

Example #2: Genesis 2:21

וַיַּפֵּל֩ יְהֹוָ֨ה אֱלֹהִ֧ים ׀ תַּרְדֵּמָ֛ה עַל־הָֽאָדָ֖ם וַיִּישָׁ֑ן
וַיִּקַּ֗ח אַחַת֙ מִצַּלְעֹתָ֔יו וַיִּסְגֹּ֥ר בָּשָׂ֖ר תַּחְתֶּֽנָּה׃

Telisha qetannah (וַיַּפֵּל֩) joins the verb (וַיַּפֵּל֩, "caused . . . to fall" [ESV]) to the subject (יְהֹוָ֨ה אֱלֹהִ֧ים ׀, "the Lᴏʀᴅ God"). And *merekha* (וַיִּסְגֹּ֥ר) joins the verb (וַיִּסְגֹּ֥ר, "then closed up") to the direct object (בָּשָׂ֖ר, "the flesh" [NASB]).

The symbols that are the subject of this book are called "accents" because most of the time they indicate the stressed syllable in a word. Yet they are also called "sense markers" because they record an ancient interpretation of the meaning of the text. But they have one more job, and with that job comes one more name for the symbols.

JOB #3: CHANTING

The third job of the accents was to indicate how the text was to be chanted.[17] It is this third job that gives rise to the name "cantillation markers." The word "cantillation" is related to the English words "cantor," a person in the Christian church or Jewish synagogue who leads people in singing/praying/chanting, and "canticle," a hymn or chant; "cantillation" comes from the Latin word *canere* ("to sing"). Three remarks will suffice for our discussion of this third job.

---

17. "Drawing on the oral tradition, the Masoretes added to the text accent signs giving directions for its performance. The chant, that is, the intoning of the text with appropriate pauses, adds dignity, solemnity, beauty, and clarity to the reading. Each sign represents groups of notes to which the words of the verse are chanted." WO §1.6.4.a.

First, some scholars think that this is not the third job but is the first and original job of these symbols, indicating how the text was to be chanted. This is the opinion of Yeivin:

> Altogether the accents perform three functions. Their primary function . . . is to represent the musical motifs to which the Biblical text was chanted in the public reading.[18]

Price argues this position more fully:

> It is true that the placement of the disjunctive accents usually coincides with the places where syntactic divisions occur in the Hebrew language of the text, and the placement of the conjunctive accents usually coincides with the places where syntactic union occur. However, more than occasionally a disjunctive accent occurs where the syntax of Hebrew expects a union, or a conjunctive accent occurs where the syntax of Hebrew expects division. This disharmony . . . suggests that it is primarily a grammar of the music of cantillation.[19]

This opinion is supported by the idea that the chanting of the text originated in the poetry of Psalms, Job, and Proverbs. The binary nature of the majority of poetic lines in Psalms, Job, and Proverbs could lie at the heart of the binary nature of the Hebrew accents system, which will be discussed in chapter 2. From these books, the cantillation system was eventually extended to the whole of the Hebrew Bible. It is beyond the scope of this introductory book to enter into this discussion; my order of "accents," "sense markers," and "cantillation markers" is pragmatic. The first thing students need help with is knowing where to stress each word as the text is read. Then students need help in knowing how to batch the text into sense units. The listing of the cantillation job is third here, especially in light of the next remark.

---

18. Yeivin, *Introduction to the Tiberian Masorah*, 158.
19. Price, *Concordance of the Hebrew Accents*, 1.19–21.

Second, we do not have access to the masoretic signification of the "cantillation markers."[20] "The precise musical contour denoted by the various Tiberian accent signs is unknown."[21] Moreover, "it is not clear what relation the surviving cantillation traditions of the various Jewish communities have with the Tiberian system."[22]

Nowadays different communities (Ashkenazic, Sephardic, Babylonian, Yemenite, etc.) use different chants in their synagogue readings. . . . There is no way of telling the extent to which these chants now in use reflect that used in Israel when the accent signs were fixed by the Tiberian Masoretes. . . .[23]

"The variety of pronunciations among various Jewish communities signals that caution must be used in absolutizing any one accentual system. . . ."[24] Given that we do not know how the ancient text was chanted, we will not devote further space to this discussion.

Third, the final job of indicating how the text was chanted was no doubt related to how the text was interpreted. Or to put it another way, the jobs of the "cantillation markers" and the "sense markers" were intertwined.

This chant enhanced the beauty and solemnity of the reading, but because the purpose of the reading was to present the text clearly and intelligibly to the hearers, the chant is dependent on the text, and emphasizes the logical relationships of the words.[25]

A knowledge of the masoretic chanting system would no doubt serve to confirm our knowledge of the sense divisions of the text.

---

20. Davis, *The Hebrew Accents of the Twenty-One Books of the Bible*, 13; WO, 30; Yeivin, *Introduction to the Tiberian Masorah*, 159.

21. Geoffrey Khan, *A Short Introduction to the Tiberian Masoretic Bible and Its Reading Tradition*, 2nd ed. (Piscataway, NJ: Gorgias, 2014), 37.

22. Khan, *A Short Introduction*, 37.

23. Yeivin, *Introduction to the Tiberian Masorah*, 159; see also Lehman, *Reading with the Masoretes*, 9n13, "Numerous modern interpretations of the tropes exist within these general geographic groupings: Ashkenazic, Sephardic, Moroccan, Egyptian, Syrian, Baghdadian, and Yemenite. Each cantillation system exhibits elements of its own historical and geographic development.

24. WO, 30.

25. Yeivin, *Introduction to the Tiberian Masorah*, 158.

With this basic understanding of the three jobs of the "accents," "sense markers," and "cantillation markers" in clear view, the following two chapters will be devoted to deepening our understanding of the "sense markers" so as to enhance our ability to read the text with understanding.

OTHER MASORETIC MARKS

Before leaving this chapter, let's discuss four miscellaneous items that are not accents but are closely related to the accent system.

The first is *soph pasuq* (סוֹף פָּסוּק). *Soph pasuq* means "end of verse" and refers to what looks like a colon composed of two diamonds[26] placed after the final word of a verse, as in הָאָֽרֶץ׃ ("the earth," Gen 1:1). While some scholars treat *soph pasuq* as part of the accent system,[27] I along with others do not treat *soph pasuq* as an accent.[28] One reason is that *soph pasuq* does not have the job of marking the stressed syllable of a word, since it does not occur above or below a syllable as all other accents do. Another reason is that *soph pasuq* was not used consistently in ancient manuscripts to the degree that *silluq* was.[29] The accent on the final word of a verse is therefore *silluq*, which is then followed by *soph pasuq*.[30]

The second is *maqqeph* (מַקֵּף). *Maqqeph* looks like a hyphen, but it is raised above midline, as in וַֽיְהִי־אֽוֹר ("and there was light," Gen 1:3). Where multiple words are joined together into one accentual unit, they are joined by *maqqeph*. Like *soph pasuq*, *maqqeph* is not an accent, as it plays no role in showing stress or in chanting the text.[31] Most of the time *maqqeph* joins two words together, but it may join three and even four. It is usually the case that words joined by *maqqeph* have only one accent, but occasionally

---

26. In ancient manuscripts, *soph pasuq* was represented by either two dots or just one dot.

27. See, for example, Fuller and Choi, *Hebrew Syntax*, 356; Price, *Concordance of the Hebrew Accents*, 1.23.

28. See, for example, Davis, *The Hebrew Accents of the Twenty-One Books of the Bible*, 2.4; Lehman, *Reading with the Masoretes*, 83n9; Yeivin, *Introduction to the Tiberian Masorah*, 208.

29. Yeivin, *Introduction to the Tiberian Masorah*, 176.

30. This discussion is complicated by the fact that at times *silluq* has been called *soph pasuq*; see Yeivin, *Introduction to the Tiberian Masorah*, 176.

31. Yeivin, *Introduction to the Tiberian Masorah*, 228.

the first word in the unit can have a conjunctive accent, as in וַתֹּאמֶר־אֶסְתֵּ֔ר ("Esther said," Esth 7:6).[32]

The third is *paseq* (פָּסֵק). *Paseq* is a vertical line that occurs immediately following a word, as in וַיִּקְרָ֣א אֱלֹהִים| ("and God said," Gen 1:3). *Paseq* follows a word with a conjunctive accent and indicates the need for a slight pause, but not a pause that warrants a disjunctive accent,[33] and is used to slightly separate words for one reason or another.[34] Owing to its frequent combination with a couple of disjunctive accents,[35] *paseq* can be thought of as part of the accent system, though not as an independent symbol.

The fourth miscellaneous item is pausal forms. A pausal form is a form of a word where there is, for example, a slight lengthening of a vowel in the shift from a short *patakh* to a medium *qamets*, owing to the pause in reading and generated by a disjunctive accent. In general, pausal forms are generated by *silluq* and *atnakh*, but they may also occur with other accents like *segolta* and *zaqeph*. For example, the lexical form of "water" is מַיִם, and in the pausal form the *qamets* replaces *patakh*, as in הַמָּיִם (Gen 1:6).

Now that we have met the accents and learned their three basic jobs, we can turn our attention to the details of how the accents are used.

---

32. For a detailed description of the use of *maqqeph*, see Yeivin, *Introduction to the Tiberian Masorah*, 230–36.

33. Yeivin, *Introduction to the Tiberian Masorah*, 216.

34. For detailed discussions, see Yeivin, *Introduction to the Tiberian Masorah*, 216–17; Wickes, *A Treatise on the Twenty-One*, 122–29.

35. For example, *legarmeh* (כָּל־נֶ֣פֶשׁ הַֽחַיָּ֞ה|, "and every living thing" in Gen 1:21) is composed of *munakh* + *paseq*.

CHAPTER 2

THE ACCENTS AND SENSE, PART ONE:

The Disjunctive Accents

The second job of the accents is to indicate the sense of the text by showing the syntactic relationships between words. The accents fall into two groups: those that divide words (disjunctive accents) and those that join words (conjunctive accents). In this chapter, you are studying only the disjunctive accents. The conjunctive accents will be the topic of the following chapter.

Hebrew tradition refers to the disjunctive accents as "kings" (מְלָכִים) and to the conjunctive accents as "servants" (מְשָׁרְתִים). You may encounter this Hebrew tradition under the Latin names *reges* or *domini* ("kings" or "lords") and *servi* ("servants"). Following this Hebrew tradition of referring to the disjunctive accents as "kings" (מְלָכִים), Christian scholars[1] as early as the 1600s divided the disjunctive accents into emperors, kings, princes, dukes, and counts.[2] While there has been a resurgence of this approach among some Christian and Jewish scholars,[3] not all are agreed that this is the best approach.[4] About this nomenclature, Gesenius said,

> The division of the disjunctive accents into Imperatores, Reges, Duces, Comites, which became common amongst Christian grammarians . . . as the source of manifold confusion, had better be given up.[5]

---

1. Yeivin, *Introduction to the Tiberian Masorah*, 168–69.
2. "Following the work of Bohlius in the Lutheran University at Rostock (Scrutinium Sanct. Scr. ex accentibus, 1636) it became fashionable among Christian hebraists to divide the 'kings' into a hierarchically structured 'ruling class' consisting of Imperatores, Reges, Duces, Comites etc." Robinson and Levy, "The Masoretes and the Punctuation of Biblical Hebrew," 10–11.
3. For a recent example, see Fuller and Choi, *Hebrew Syntax*, 351–413.
4. "While this system is very graphic and is a very useful teaching aid, it does not convey what actually happens in the text." Robinson and Levy, "The Masoretes and the Punctuation of Biblical Hebrew," 11.
5. GKC, 59n1.

In a similar way, Wickes referred to this nomenclature as a "fanciful division" that should be dispensed with.[6] And Yeivin said, "indeed it does give a false impression of the accent system."[7] While these may be overstatements of the case, they show that there are differing opinions on how to describe the accents as markers of the sense of the text. Though I follow a different method of presentation[8] and do not use the language of emperors, kings, princes, etc., I find much that is helpful in the works of those who take this approach.[9] And in spite of his criticism, Yeivin himself says, "The divisions of the accents into four grades can, however, provide a useful guide."[10]

There are twenty-seven different accents for the Twenty-One.[11] Eighteen of these are disjunctive. These eighteen can be divided into four groups based on their hierarchical strength, and within each group there is a sliding scale of strength.[12] So before moving on to a fuller discussion of how the disjunctive accents work, let's review them with a focus on the groups into which they can be batched.

THE GROUPS OF THE DISJUNCTIVE ACCENTS

Group 1[13]

Hebrew Name	English Name	Symbol	Symbol
סִלּוּק	silluq	טטט	ֽ
אַתְנָח	atnakh	טטט	֑

---

6. William Wickes, *A Treatise on the Accentuation of the Three So-Called Poetical Books on the Old Testament, Psalms, Proverbs, and Job* (Leopold Classic Library, 1881; repr., Oxford: Clarendon), 11.

7. Yeivin, *Introduction to the Tiberian Masorah*, 169.

8. See David Robinson and Elisabeth Levy, "Masoretic Hebrew Cantillation and Constituent Structure Analysis," *British & Foreign Bible Society* (May 2, 2002), http://lc.bfbs.org.uk/e107_files/downloads/masoretes.pdf; Robinson and Levy, "The Masoretes and the Punctuation of Biblical Hebrew."

9. See especially Fuller and Choi, *Hebrew Syntax*, 351–413.

10. Yeivin, *Introduction to the Tiberian Masorah*, 169.

11. That is, all of the books except Psalms, (the poetic section of) Job, and Proverbs, which have a related but different system and are referred to as the Three books.

12. Davis, *The Hebrew Accents of the Twenty-One Books of the Bible*, 2.3.

13. My group 1 are the "kings."

Group 2[14]

Hebrew Name	English Name	Symbol	Symbol
סְגוֹלְתָּא	segolta	טטּ	֯
שַׁלְשֶׁלֶת	shalshelet	טטּ|	֓|
זָקֵף קָטוֹן	zaqeph qaton	טטֵ	֔
זָקֵף גָּדוֹל	zaqeph gadol	טטֵ	֕
טִפְחָה	tiphkha	טטֶ	֖

Group 3[15]

Hebrew Name	English Name	Symbol	Symbol
רְבִיעַ	revia	טטֵ	֗
זַרְקָא	zarqa	טטֵ	֘
פַּשְׁטָא	pashta	טטֵ	֙
תְּבִיר	tevir	טטֶ	֛
יְתִיב	yetiv	טטֶ	֚

Group 4[16]

Hebrew Name	English Name	Symbol	Symbol
פָּזֵר	pazer	טטֵ	֡
קַרְנֵי פָּרָה	qarne parah	טטֵ	֟
תְּלִישָׁה גְדוֹלָה	telishah gedolah	טטֵ	֠
גֶּרֶשׁ	geresh	טטֵ	֜
גֵּרְשַׁיִם	gershayim	טטֵ	֞
לְגַרְמֶה	legarmeh	טטֶ|	֩|

---

14. My group 2 are the "princes."
15. My group 3 are the "dukes."
16. My group 4 are the "counts."

At its heart, the accent system is binary,[17] and the disjunctive accents work on the principle of "continuous dichotomy,"[18] that is, the dividing of a verse in half, then half of the half in half, then half of the half of the half, etc.

In general, accents in a given group are divided in half by accents in the group below. So accents in group 1 are divided by accents in group 2, accents in group 2 are divided by accents in group 3, and accents in group 3 are divided by accents in group 4.[19] There is more to it than this, but this is a picture of the forest to keep in mind so that you do not get lost in the trees.

There is a general pattern of dividing verses with the disjunctive accents. First, the end of a verse is marked by an accent. Second, a verse is divided in half by a different accent. Third, each half verse is divided in half by

---

17. "By the end of the seventh century the highly advanced mathematics of India had spread to northern Mesopotamia where it was eagerly embraced by Islamic scholars. In the early ninth century the House of Wisdom was built in Baghdad, near Nehardea. This was on the one hand a centre for translation and preservation of ancient texts (particularly the major Greek mathematical writings) but it was also here that Islamic mathematics flowered. Perhaps its most influential scholar was al-Khwarizmi whose name gave us the word *algorithm* and one of whose works coined the word *algebra* (*al-jabr*, 'restoring'). Among many innovations he developed the new mathematics of decimal fractions and *binary* (emphasis added) division to calculate the time when the new moon would be first visible and the direction of Mecca, thus binding Islamic religion and science inseparably. More significantly for our present purposes, al-Khwarizmi also established mathematical models for the very complex Muslim rules of inheritance, which were also binding on Jewish exiles in Islamic territory. This applied to all the Jewish academies since even Tiberias was now under Islamic control. Mathematics, to some degree at least, was now an essential tool for both Jewish and Muslim religious scholars. There is no direct evidence that the Masoretes were trained in mathematics, but the probability seems substantial. The *binary* (emphasis added) division and subdivision of the text of scripture rapidly became the focus of their punctuation, which combined traditional musical notation with a consistent *binary* (emphasis added) analysis of the constituents of every verse of scripture." Robinson and Levy, "The Masoretes and the Punctuation of Biblical Hebrew," 7–8.

18. Wickes, *A Treatise on the Accentuation of the Twenty-One*, 2.29.

19. "The difference between the scheme proposed here and the earlier gradings into 'emperors, kings, etc.,' is that the pausal value of the grades in this scheme is relative, not absolute. I.e. disjunctives of grade II are not characterized by a longer pause than those of grade III, but by the fact that their clause is normally divided by a disjunctive of grade III. For this reason, in a short verse, the real disjunctive value (in terms of ordinary syntax) of a disjunctive of grade II might be less than that of a disjunctive of grade IV in a long verse or in different circumstances. Furthermore, because of the requirements of the music of the chant, some major disjunctives must be proceeded by particular minor disjunctives. For this reason minor disjunctives (e.g. grade III) may come to fill a position in which, from the point of view of syntax, a disjunctive of a superior grade (e.g. grade II) might be expected." Yeivin, *Introduction to the Tiberian Masorah*, 169.

other accents, and so on, until the whole verse is divided up. These divisions are not based on word count but on the sense of the text. Sometimes, for example, a verse contains two main clauses introduced by *waw*-consecutive imperfect verbs, and each half of the verse contains one of those clauses.

Example #1: Genesis 1:3

וַיִּֽהִי־אֽוֹר׃	וַיֹּ֥אמֶר אֱלֹהִ֖ים יְהִ֣י א֑וֹר
and there was light.	And God said, "Let there be light,"

Example #2: Genesis 1:4

וַיַּבְדֵּ֣ל אֱלֹהִ֔ים בֵּ֥ין הָא֖וֹר וּבֵ֥ין הַחֹֽשֶׁךְ׃	וַיַּ֧רְא אֱלֹהִ֛ים אֶת־הָא֖וֹר כִּי־ט֑וֹב
And God separated the light from the darkness.	And God saw the light, that it was good.

At other times, a verse contains a single clause, and the major division separates the predicate and subject from the direct object or the main clause from the subordinate clause.

Example #3: Genesis 1:1

אֵ֥ת הַשָּׁמַ֖יִם וְאֵ֥ת הָאָֽרֶץ׃	בְּרֵאשִׁ֖ית בָּרָ֣א אֱלֹהִ֑ים
the heavens and the earth.	In the beginning God created

Example #4: Genesis 3:23

לַֽעֲבֹד֙ אֶת־הָ֣אֲדָמָ֔ה אֲשֶׁ֥ר לֻקַּ֖ח מִשָּֽׁם׃	וַֽיְשַׁלְּחֵ֛הוּ יְהוָ֥ה אֱלֹהִ֖ים מִגַּן־עֵ֑דֶן
to work the ground which he had been taken from there.	So the LORD God sent him from the garden of Eden

With the principle of "continuous dichotomy" in mind, we are in a position to look at the disjunctive accents in detail in terms of what their particular jobs are and how they relate to each other. Let's begin with the major disjunctive accents and then move on to the minor ones.

THE MAJOR DISJUNCTIVE
ACCENTS AT WORK

By major disjunctive accents I am referring to those in group 1 and group 2. If the only thing you learn about the Hebrew accents is how these major disjunctive accents work, your ability to read the Hebrew Bible will be significantly enhanced, and your investment of time and energy will be richly rewarded.

Group 1: *Silluq* ֧ and *Atnakh* ֑

SILLUQ ֧

Silluq ֧ always occurs on the very last word of a verse, and it divides one verse from another.

Example #1: Genesis 1:1

בְּרֵאשִׁית בָּרָא אֱלֹהִים אֵת הַשָּׁמַיִם וְאֵת הָאָרֶץ׃

In the beginning God created the heavens and the earth.

Example #2: Genesis 1:3

וַיֹּאמֶר אֱלֹהִים יְהִי אוֹר וַיְהִי־אוֹר׃

And God said, "Let there be light," and there was light.

Silluq ֗ marks the end of Genesis 1:1 (הָאָרֶץ) and 1:3 (אוֹר).

ATNAKH ֑

Atnakh ֑ divides a verse in half, not in terms of word count but in terms of sense.

Example #1: Genesis 1:2

וְהָאָרֶץ הָיְתָה תֹהוּ וָבֹהוּ
וְחֹשֶׁךְ עַל־פְּנֵי תְהוֹם
וְרוּחַ אֱלֹהִים מְרַחֶפֶת עַל־פְּנֵי הַמָּיִם׃

Now the earth was formless and empty,

darkness was over the surface of the deep,

and the spirit of God was hovering over the waters.

Atnakh ֪ divides this verse in half by separating the two negative conditions ("formless and empty, darkness was over the surface of the deep") from the positive condition ("the spirit of God was hovering over the waters").

Example #2: Genesis 1:27

וַיִּבְרָ֨א אֱלֹהִ֤ים ׀ אֶת־הָֽאָדָם֙ בְּצַלְמ֔וֹ

בְּצֶ֥לֶם אֱלֹהִ֖ים בָּרָ֣א אֹת֑וֹ

זָכָ֥ר וּנְקֵבָ֖ה בָּרָ֥א אֹתָֽם׃

So God created mankind in his own image,

in the image of God he created them;

male and female he created them.

Atnakh ֪ divides this verse in half by separating the affirmation that God created humanity in his image from the affirmation that God created humanity male and female.

By dividing a verse in half, *atnakh* provides an unintended benefit for those reading the Hebrew Bible, especially beginners. *Atnakh* divides a verse into two chunks, and analyzing each smaller chunk separately is much easier than tackling an entire verse. Once the two chunks or half verses have been analyzed, the reader can put them together for an understanding of the whole verse.

Group 2: *Segolta* ֒ and *Shalshelet* ׀֓, *Zaqeph Qaton* ֔ and *Zaqeph Gadol* ֕, and *Tiphkha* ֖

In general, accents in group 2 divide in half units created by accents in group 1.

SEGOLTA ֒

Segolta ֒ divides the first half of a verse in half,[20] but is never used after *atnakh*, that is, *segolta* is never used to divide the second half of a verse

---

20. Based on the principle of continuous dichotomy, this is the model that I use, but I am not certain that this is always the case. It seems that at least in some texts *segolta* marks the end of the first third of the verse, with *atnakh* marking the end of the second third and *silluq* marking the end of the

in half. In addition, *segolta* is not used with high frequency, being found only in longer verses. For example, *segolta* is used in Genesis 1:1–2:3 only two times (Gen 1:7, 28).

Example #1: Genesis 1:7

וַיַּ֤עַשׂ אֱלֹהִים֙ אֶת־הָרָקִ֔יעַ

וַיַּבְדֵּ֗ל בֵּ֤ין הַמַּ֙יִם֙ אֲשֶׁר֙ מִתַּ֣חַת לָרָקִ֔יעַ וּבֵ֣ין הַמַּ֔יִם אֲשֶׁ֖ר מֵעַ֣ל לָרָקִ֑יעַ

וַֽיְהִי־כֵֽן׃

So God made the vault

and separated the water under the vault from the water above the vault.

And it was so.

This verse is divided in half by *atnakh* (לָרָקִ֑יעַ), with the first half consisting of God's actions ("made" and "separated") and the second half providing a summary ("And it was so."). The first half is then divided in half by *segolta* (אֶת־הָרָקִ֔יעַ), which separates the first *waw*-consecutive imperfect clause (וַיַּ֤עַשׂ, "made") from the second *waw*-consecutive imperfect clause (וַיַּבְדֵּ֗ל, "separated").

Example #2: Genesis 1:28

וַיְבָ֣רֶךְ אֹתָם֮ אֱלֹהִים֒

וַיֹּ֨אמֶר לָהֶ֜ם אֱלֹהִ֗ים

פְּר֥וּ וּרְב֛וּ וּמִלְא֥וּ אֶת־הָאָ֖רֶץ וְכִבְשֻׁ֑הָ

וּרְד֞וּ בִּדְגַ֤ת הַיָּם֙ וּבְע֣וֹף הַשָּׁמַ֔יִם

וּבְכָל־חַיָּ֖ה הָֽרֹמֶ֥שֶׂת עַל־הָאָֽרֶץ׃

God blessed them

and God said to them,

"Be fruitful and increase in number; fill the earth and subdue it.

Rule over the fish in the sea and the birds in the sky

and over every living creature that moves on the ground."

---

last third. Some older scholars take it to be the case that *segolta* always marks the first third of a verse; so Davis, *The Hebrew Accents of the Twenty-One Books of the Bible*, 2.13; Yeivin, *Introduction to the Tiberian Masorah*, 171, for older scholars who take this position, but note that Yeivin does not himself take this position.

This verse is divided in half by *atnakh* (וְכִבְשֻׁהָ). The first half is then divided in half by *segolta* (אֱלֹהִים), which separates the first *waw*-consecutive imperfect clause (וַיְבָרֶךְ, "blessed") from the second *waw*-consecutive imperfect clause (וַיֹּאמֶר, "said"); this second *waw*-consecutive imperfect clause is epexegetical, or explanatory,[21] as it articulates the way in which God blessed humanity: "by saying."

SHALSHELET |֓

Shalshelet |֓ is a substitute for *segolta* and occurs only fourteen times in the Twenty-One. So, if you encounter *shalshelet*, think of it as *segolta*.

ZAQEPH QATON ֔

Zaqeph qaton ֔ is statistically the most common accent used to divide a half verse in half, and unlike *segolta*, *zaqeph* is used to divide both the first and the second halves of a verse in half.

Example #1: Genesis 1:2

וְהָאָרֶץ הָיְתָה תֹהוּ וָבֹהוּ
וְחֹשֶׁךְ עַל־פְּנֵי תְהוֹם
וְרוּחַ אֱלֹהִים מְרַחֶפֶת עַל־פְּנֵי הַמָּיִם:

Now the earth was formless and empty,
darkness was over the surface of the deep,
and the spirit of God was hovering over the waters.

As we saw earlier, *atnakh* (תְהוֹם) divides this verse in half, separating the two negative conditions ("formless and empty, darkness was over the surface of the deep") from the one positive condition ("the spirit of God was hovering over the waters"). *Zaqeph* (וָבֹהוּ) then divides the first half of the verse in half, separating the first negative condition ("formless and empty") from the second ("darkness was over the surface of the deep"). Then *zaqeph* (אֱלֹהִים) divides the second half of the verse in half, separating the subject ("the spirit of God") from the predicate ("was hovering over the waters").

---

21. Joüon §118j; WO §33.2.2.

Example #2: Genesis 1:16

וַיַּעַשׂ אֱלֹהִים אֶת־שְׁנֵי הַמְּאֹרֹת הַגְּדֹלִים
אֶת־הַמָּאוֹר הַגָּדֹל לְמֶמְשֶׁלֶת הַיּוֹם
וְאֶת־הַמָּאוֹר הַקָּטֹן לְמֶמְשֶׁלֶת הַלַּיְלָה
וְאֵת הַכּוֹכָבִים׃

God made two great lights—
the greater light to govern the day
and the lesser light to govern the night.
He also made the stars. (NIV)

This verse is divided in half by *atnakh* (הַגְּדֹלִים), separating the predicate ("made"), subject ("God"), and direct object ("two great lights") from the amplification of the direct object ("the greater light to govern the day and the lesser light to govern the night. He also made the stars"). Note how the NIV captures this major division with the use of the em dash after "great lights." The first half of this verse is then divided in half by *zaqeph* (אֱלֹהִים), which separates the predicate and subject ("God made") from the direct object ("two great lights").

Note that the second half of the verse uses *zaqeph* twice, once on הַיּוֹם ("the day") and then on הַלַּיְלָה ("the night"). Whenever *zaqeph* is repeated in a half verse, the first *zaqeph* is the one that divides the half in half;[22] the second *zaqeph* divides the second half of the half in half. That being said, the first *zaqeph* separates the greater light that rules the day from the lesser light and the stars that shine at night. Though it is not a major point, the NIV[23] presents a different interpretation of the text, as it places the reference to the stars in a separate sentence ("He also made the stars."). The ESV likewise separates out the reference to the stars with its use of an em dash ("—and the stars"). These translations lead the reader to take the creation of the stars almost as an afterthought, which may be correct but is not the interpretation of the ancient Masoretes, who have encoded an interpretation

---

22. Fuller and Choi, *Hebrew Syntax*, 359n11; Yeivin, *Introduction to the Tiberian Masorah*, 170.
23. So too the NLT.

far closer to the original community than our own. According to this ancient interpretation, the stars are joined to the lesser light and implicitly share in the rule of the night. If the intention were to separate the stars from the two great lights, we might expect *atnakh* on הַלַּיְלָה ("the night"). This interpretation comports with Psalm 136:9a, "the moon and stars to govern the night."

ZAQEPH GADOL ◌̊

Zaqeph gadol ◌̊ is a substitute for *zaqeph qaton*. If you encounter *zaqeph gadol*, think of it as *zaqeph qaton*.

TIPHKHA ◌̣

Tiphkha ◌̣ is a bit more multifaceted than the accents studied to this point. First, when *tiphkha* occurs, it is always the final disjunctive accent before *silluq* or *atnakh*. Second, in shorter half verses *tiphkha*, not *zaqeph*, divides the half in half, while in longer half verses *tiphkha* divides the unit following *zaqeph* in half.

Example #1: Genesis 1:1

אֵת הַשָּׁמַיִם וְאֵת הָאָרֶץ:	בְּרֵאשִׁית בָּרָא אֱלֹהִים
the heavens and the earth.	In the beginning God created

In both half verses, *tiphkha* is the final disjunctive accent before *silluq* and *atnakh*, respectively. In addition, *tiphkha* divides both of these short half verses in half. In the first, *tiphkha* separates the prepositional phrase ("In the beginning") from the predicate and subject ("God created"), while in the second, *tiphkha* separates the first half of the direct object ("the heavens") from the second half ("the earth").

Example #2: Genesis 1:3a

יְהִי אוֹר	וַיֹּאמֶר אֱלֹהִים
Let there be light	And God said

In this half verse, *tiphkha* (אֱלֹהִ֔ים) is the final disjunctive accent before *atnakh*. In addition, *tiphkha* divides this short half verse in half, separating the introduction to speech ("And God said") from the speech itself ("Let there be light.").

Example #3: Genesis 1:4b

בֵּ֥ין הָא֖וֹר וּבֵ֥ין הַחֹֽשֶׁךְ׃	וַיַּבְדֵּ֣ל אֱלֹהִ֔ים
between the light and between the darkness	Then God separated

In this half verse, *tiphkha* (הָא֖וֹר) is the final disjunctive accent before *silluq*. In addition, *tiphkha* divides the unit following *zaqeph* in half, separating the first prepositional phrase ("between the light") from the second prepositional phrase ("and between the darkness").

Example #4: Genesis 1:6

וִיהִ֣י מַבְדִּ֔יל בֵּ֥ין מַ֖יִם לָמָֽיִם׃	וַיֹּ֣אמֶר אֱלֹהִ֗ים יְהִ֤י רָקִ֙יעַ֙ בְּת֣וֹךְ הַמָּ֔יִם
And let it be separating between water to water."	And God said, "Let there be a vault between the waters.

In both of these half verses, *tiphkha* is the last disjunctive accent before *silluq* and *atnakh*. In the first half-verse, *tiphkha* (רָקִ֙יעַ֙) separates the unit following *zaqeph* ("Let there be a vault between the waters") in half by separating the predicate and the subject ("Let there be a vault") from the prepositional modifier ("between the waters"). In the second half-verse, *tiphkha* (מַ֖יִם) separates the unit following *zaqeph* ("between water to water") in half by separating the first prepositional modifier ("between water") from the second prepositional modifier ("to water").

By way of summary we can say that the group 1 accents—*silluq* and *atnakh*—are the two major disjunctive accents:

1. *Silluq* divides one verse from another.
2. *Atnakh* divides a verse in half.

In general, it can be said that the group 2 accents—*segolta*, *zaqeph*, and *tiphkha*—divide a half-verse in half:

1. *Segolta* can divide the first half of long verses in half.
   - *Shalshelet* is a substitute for *segolta*.
2. *Zaqeph qaton* is the typical accent that divides both the first and the second halves of a verse in half.
   - *Zaqeph gadol* is a substitute for *zaqeph qaton*.
3. *Tiphkha* is always the final disjunctive accent before *silluq* and *atnakh* and can divide a unit following *zaqeph* in half. *Tiphkha* can divide a short half-verse in half.

THE MINOR DISJUNCTIVE ACCENTS AT WORK

By minor disjunctive accents I am referring to those in group 3 and group 4. Since this is only an introduction to the Hebrew accents system, which does not intend to be exhaustive but intends to provide an entrée into the accent system, we will refer to all of the disjunctive accents in group 3 and group 4 but will only illustrate the more frequent ones.

Group 3: *Revia* ȯ, *Zarqa* ȏ, *Pashta* ȯ and *Tevir* ọ, and *Yetiv* ọ

In general, accents in group 3 divide in half units created by accents in group 2.

Revia ȯ

Revia ȯ divides in half a unit created by a group 2 accent. Let's look at some examples with *segolta*, *zaqeph*, and *tiphkha*.

Example #1: Genesis 3:17

כִּי־שָׁמַעְתָּ לְקוֹל אִשְׁתֶּךָ	וּלְאָדָם אָמַר
"Because you listened to your wife . . ."	And to Adam he said

Here *revia* (אָמַר) divides a *segolta* unit in half by separating the introduction to speech ("And to Adam he said") from the speech itself ("Because you listened to your wife").

Example #2: Genesis 28:6

כִּי־בֵרַךְ יִצְחָק אֶת־יַעֲקֹב	וַיַּרְא עֵשָׂו
that Isaac had blessed Jacob	Then Esau saw

Here *revia* (עֵשָׂו) divides a *segolta* unit in half by separating the predicate and the subject ("Then Esau saw") from the cognate accusative ("that Isaac had blessed Jacob").

Example #3: Genesis 1:2

הָיְתָה תֹהוּ וָבֹהוּ	וְהָאָרֶץ
was formless and empty	Now the earth

Here *revia* (וְהָאָרֶץ) divides a *zaqeph* unit in half by separating the subject ("Now the earth") from the predicate and subject complement ("was formless and empty").

Example #4: Genesis 1:14

יְהִי מְאֹרֹת בִּרְקִיעַ הַשָּׁמַיִם	וַיֹּאמֶר אֱלֹהִים
Let there be lights in the vault of the sky	And God said

Here *revia* (אֱלֹהִים) divides a *zaqeph* unit in half by separating the introduction to speech ("And God said") from the speech itself ("Let there be lights in the vault of the sky").

Example #5: Genesis 3:11

אֲשֶׁר צִוִּיתִיךָ לְבִלְתִּי אֲכָל־מִמֶּנּוּ	הֲמִן־הָעֵץ
which I commanded you not to eat from it	from the tree

Here *revia* (הֲמִן־הָעֵץ) divides a *tiphkha* unit in half by separating the prepositional phrase ("from the tree") from the modifying relative clause ("which I commanded you not to eat from it").

Example #6: Genesis 7:2

תִּקַּח־לְךָ֖ שִׁבְעָ֣ה שִׁבְעָ֔ה	מִכֹּ֣ל ׀ הַבְּהֵמָ֣ה הַטְּהוֹרָ֗ה
Take for yourself seven pairs	From all of the clean animals

Here *revia* (הַטְּהוֹרָ֗ה) divides a *tiphkha* unit in half by separating the prepositional phrase ("From all of the clean animals") from the predicate and direct object ("Take for yourself seven pairs").

ZARQA ◌֮

Zarqa ◌֮ occurs only in a unit created by *segolta*. Being a group 3 accent, *zarqa* is in the same group as *revia*, but *zarqa* is not as strong as *revia*. Typically, a *segolta* unit is divided in half by *revia*, but in the absence of *revia*, *zarqa* can divide a short *segolta* unit in half.

Example #1: Genesis 1:7

אֶת־הָרָקִ֘יעַ֮	וַיַּ֣עַשׂ אֱלֹהִים֮
the vault	So God made

Here *zarqa* (אֱלֹהִים֮) divides a *segolta* unit in half by separating the predicate and the subject ("So God made") from the direct object ("the vault").

Example #2: Genesis 1:28

אֱלֹהִים֒	וַיְבָ֣רֶךְ אֹתָם֮
God	blessed them

Here *zarqa* (אֹתָם֮) divides a *segolta* unit in half by separating the predicate and direct object ("blessed them") from the subject ("God").

If a *segolta* unit is already divided by *revia*, the second half of that unit can be subdivided by *zarqa*.

Example #3: Genesis 3:17

כִּי־שָׁמַ֫עְתָּ֮ לְק֣וֹל אִשְׁתֶּךָ֒	וּלְאָדָ֣ם אָמַ֗ר
Because you listened to your wife	To Adam he said

This *segolta* unit is divided in half by *revia* (אָמַר), which separates the introduction of the speech ("To Adam he said") from the speech itself ("Because you listened to your wife"). Then the second half of the *segolta* unit is divided in half by *zarqa* (כִּי־שָׁמַעְתָּ֩), which separates the predicate ("Because you listened") from the indirect object ("to your wife").

Example #4: Genesis 22:9

אֶל־הַמָּקוֹם֙ אֲשֶׁר אָמַר־לֹ֥ו הָאֱלֹהִ֑ים	וַיָּבֹ֗אוּ
the place God had told them about	When they reached

This *segolta* unit is divided in half by *revia* (וַיָּבֹ֗אוּ), which separates the predicate ("When they reached") from the indirect object ("the place God had told them about"). Then the second half of the *segolta* unit is divided in half by *zarqa* (אֶל־הַמָּקוֹם֙), which separates the prepositional phrase ("the place") from the modifying relative clause ("God had told them about").

Pashta ׇֹ

Pashta ׇֹ occurs only in a unit created by *zaqeph*. Being a group 3 accent, *pashta* is in the same group as *revia and zarqa*, but *pashta* is not as strong as *revia* or *zarqa*. Typically, a *zaqeph* unit is divided in half by *revia*, but in the absence of *revia*, *pashta* can divide a short *zaqeph* unit in half.

Example #1: Genesis 1:5

י֖וֹם	וַיִּקְרָ֨א אֱלֹהִ֤ים׀ לָאוֹר֙
day	God called the light

This *zaqeph* unit is divided in half by *pashta* (לָאוֹר֙), which separates the predicate, subject, and indirect object ("God called the light") from the direct object ("day").

Example #2: Genesis 1:20

יְעוֹפֵ֣ף עַל־הָאָ֑רֶץ	וְע֣וֹף
let fly above the earth	And birds

This *zaqeph* unit is divided in half by *pashta* (וְעוֹף), which separates the subject ("And birds") from the predicate ("let fly above the earth").

If a *zaqeph* unit is already divided by *revia*, the second half of that unit can be divided by *pashta*.

Example #3: Genesis 1:2

הָיְתָה תֹהוּ וָבֹהוּ[24]	וְהָאָרֶץ
was formless and empty	Now the earth

This[24] *zaqeph* unit is divided in half by *revia* (וְהָאָרֶץ), which separates the subject ("Now the earth") from the predicate and subject complements ("was formless and empty"). Then the second half of the *zaqeph* unit is divided in half by *pashta* (תֹהוּ), which separates the predicate and the first subject complement ("was formless") from the second subject complement ("and empty").

Example #4: Genesis 1:11

תַּדְשֵׁא הָאָרֶץ דֶּשֶׁא	וַיֹּאמֶר אֱלֹהִים
Let the land produce vegetation	Then God said

This *zaqeph* unit is divided in half by *revia* (אֱלֹהִים), which separates the introduction to the speech ("Then God said") from the speech itself ("Let the land produce vegetation"). Then the second half of the *zaqeph* unit is divided in half by *pashta* (הָאָרֶץ), which separates the predicate and the subject ("Let the land produce") from the direct object ("vegetation").

TEVIR ◌

Tevir ◌ occurs only in a unit created by *tiphkha*. Being a group 3 accent, *tevir* is in the same group as *revia*, *zarqa*, and *pashta*, but *tevir* is not as strong as *revia*, *zarqa*, or *pashta*. Typically, a *tiphkha* unit is divided in half by *revia*, but in the absence of *revia*, *tevir* can divide a short *tiphkha* unit in half.

---

24. Remember that *pashta* is postpositive, and when the last syllable is not accented, *pashta* is repeated on the accented syllable.

Example #1: Genesis 1:4

אֶת־הָאֽוֹר	וַיַּ֧רְא אֱלֹהִ֛ים
the light	God saw

This *tiphkha* unit is divided in half by *tevir* (אֱלֹהִ֛ים), which separates the predicate and subject ("God saw") from the direct object ("the light").

Example #2: Genesis 1:22

אֱלֹהִ֖ים	וַיְבָ֧רֶךְ אֹתָ֛ם
God	blessed them

This *tiphkha* unit is divided in half by *tevir* (אֹתָ֛ם), which separates the predicate and direct object ("blessed them") from the subject ("God").

If a *tiphkha* unit is already divided by *revia*, the second half of that unit can be subdivided by *tevir*.

Example #3: Genesis 1:28

פְּר֧וּ וּרְב֛וּ וּמִלְא֥וּ אֶת־הָאָ֖רֶץ	וַיֹּ֨אמֶר לָהֶ֜ם אֱלֹהִ֗ים
Be fruitful and increase in number; fill the earth (NIV)	God said to them

This *tiphkha* unit is divided in half by *revia* (אֱלֹהִ֗ים), which separates the introduction to the speech ("God said to them") from the speech itself ("Be fruitful and increase in number; fill the earth"). Then the second half of the *tiphkha* unit is divided in half by *tevir* (וּרְב֛וּ), which separates a pair of verbs ("Be fruitful and increase in number") from the single verb ("fill the earth"). Note the sensitivity of the NIV to the accent system at this point, "Be fruitful and increase in number; fill the earth…," as it uses a semicolon to separate "be fruitful and increase in number" from "fill the earth." Being fruitful and increasing in number go together in terms of sense but are separate ideas in relation to filling the earth. One only need recall that at the time of the Tower of Babel humans were being fruitful and increasing in number, but they were not filling the earth.

Example #4: Genesis 3:11

אֲשֶׁר צִוִּיתִיךָ לְבִלְתִּי אֲכָל־מִמֶּנּוּ	הֲמִן־הָעֵץ
which I commanded you not to eat from it	from the tree

This *tiphkha* unit is divided in half by *revia* (הֲמִן־הָעֵץ), which separates the prepositional phrase ("from the tree") from the modifying relative clause ("which I commanded you not to eat from it"). Then the second half of the *tiphkha* unit is divided in half by *tevir* (צִוִּיתִיךָ), which separates the predicate ("which I commanded you) from its complement ("not to eat from it").

YETIV ֫

Yetiv ֫ is a substitute for *pashta*, so if you encounter *yetiv*, think of it as *pashta*.

By way of summary we can say that in general group 3 accents divide units created by group 2 accents in half:

1. *Revia* is the typical accent for dividing units created by *segolta*, *zaqeph*, and *tiphkha* in half.
2. *Zarqa* can divide a unit created by *segolta* in half when *revia* is absent.
3. *Pashta* can divide a unit created by *zaqeph* in half when *revia* is absent.
   • *Yetiv* is a substitute for *pashta*.
4. *Tevir* can divide a unit created by *tiphkha* in half when *revia* is absent.

When a unit created by a group 3 accent is divided in half by *revia*:

1. *Zarqa* divides the unit after *revia* and before *segolta*.
2. *Pashta* divides the unit after *revia* and before *zaqeph*.
3. *Tevir* divides the unit after *revia* and before *tiphkha*.

Group 4: Pazer ֡ and Qarne Parah ֟ or Telisha Gedolah ֠, and Geresh ֜ and Gershayim ֞, and Legarmeh |֪

In general, accents in group 4 divide in half units created by accents in group 3.

PAZER ֯

Pazer ֯ divides in half a unit created by *revia, zarqa, pashta,* or *tevir*. A couple of illustrations will suffice.

Example #1: Genesis 1:21

אֲשֶׁר֩ שָׁרְצ֨וּ הַמַּ֜יִם לְמִֽינֵהֶ֗ם	וְאֵ֣ת כָּל־נֶ֣פֶשׁ הַֽחַיָּ֣ה ׀ הָֽרֹמֶ֡שֶׂת
with which the waters swarm according to their kind	and every living thing that moves

This *revia* unit is divided in half by *pazer* (הָֽרֹמֶ֡שֶׂת), which separates the direct object ("and every living thing that moves") from the qualifying relative clause ("with which the waters swarm according to their kind").

Example #2: Genesis 22:2

קַח־נָ֣א אֶת־בִּנְךָ֙	וַיֹּ֡אמֶר
Take your son	Then he said

This *pashta* unit is divided in half by *pazer* (וַיֹּ֡אמֶר), which separates the introduction to the speech ("Then he said") from the speech itself ("take your son").

QARNE PARAH ֟

Qarne parah[25] ֟ is a substitute for *pazer*, so if you encounter *qarne parah*, think of it as *pazer*.

TELISHA GEDOLAH ֠

Telisha gedolah ֠ is a substitute for *pazer*, so if you encounter *telishah gedolah*, think of it as *pazer*.

GERESH ֜

Geresh ֜ divides in half a unit created by *revia, zarqa, pashta,* or *tevir*. A couple of illustrations will suffice.

---

25. Also called *pazer gadol*.

Example #1: Genesis 1:25

לְמִינָהּ	וַיַּעַשׂ אֱלֹהִים אֶת־חַיַּת הָאָרֶץ
according to their kinds	God made the animals of the land

This *revia* unit is divided in half by *geresh* (הָאָרֶץ), which separates the predicate, subject, and direct object ("God made the animals of the land") from the qualifying prepositional phrase ("according to their kinds").

Example #2: Genesis 1:9

מִתַּחַת הַשָּׁמַיִם	יִקָּווּ הַמַּיִם
from under the heavens	Let the waters be gathered

This *pashta* unit is divided in half by *geresh* (הַמַּיִם), which separates the predicate and subject ("Let the waters be gathered") from the prepositional phrase ("from under the heavens").

GERSHAYIM ◌֞

Gershayim ◌֞ is a substitute for *geresh* ◌֜, so if you encounter *gershayim*, think of it as *geresh*.

LEGARMEH |◌֨

Legarmeh |◌֨ typically occurs before *revia* (Gen 1:21, 30).

By way of summary we can say that in general group 4 accents divide in half units created by group 3 accents:

1. *Pazer* is the typical accent for dividing units created by *revia*, *zarqa*, *pashta*, and *tevir* in half.
   - *Qarne parah* is a substitute for *pazer*.
   - *Telishah gedolah* is a substitute for *pazer*.
2. *Geresh* can also divide in half a unit created by *revia*, *zarqa*, *pashta*, or *tevir*.
   - *Gershayim* is a substitute for *geresh*.

THE DISJUNCTIVE ACCENTS VISUALIZED

Especially as you begin to learn how to read your Hebrew Bible with the accents, but even later on when you are more adept and encounter complex verses, it will be helpful to have a way to graphically represent a verse according to the accent divisions. Let me show you three possibilities.

The system used by the Masoretes to accent the text "is in fact very similar to that used in marking constituent structure trees in linguistic analysis and can be illustrated by the same form of tree-diagram."[26] Let's take a look at Genesis 1:1 visualized as a tree-diagram.

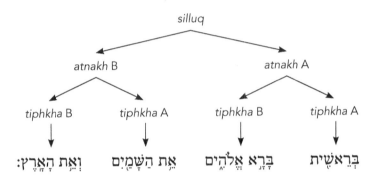

Start by looking at the bottom of the tree and you will see that the verse is divided after each disjunctive accent: *tiphkha, atnakh, tiphkha,* and *silluq*. *Silluq* governs the whole verse and so is at the top of the tree. *Atnakh* divides the verse in half. We can label the unit leading up to and including *atnakh* "*atnakh* A," and the unit following *atnakh* and terminating at *silluq* "*atnakh* B." There is nothing magical about this nomenclature. It's just a way of being able to label and talk about the units of a verse, based on the principle of continuous dichotomy. This is similar to when biblical scholars refer to the words in Genesis 1:1 up to *atnakh* as Genesis 1:1a and the words after *atnakh* up to *silluq* as Genesis 1:1b.

Atnakh A is divided by *tiphkha*, so we can label everything up to and including *tiphkha* as "*tiphkha* A" and trhe unit following *tiphkha* up to and

26. Robinson and Levy, "The Masoretes and the Punctuation of Biblical Hebrew," 11; William D. Barrick, "The Masoretic Hebrew Accents in Translation and Interpretation," n.d., http://drbarrick.org /files/papers/other/HebrewAccentsrev.pdf; Yeivin, *Introduction to the Tiberian Masorah*, 172.

including *atnakh* as "*tiphkha* B." Likewise, the *atnakh* B unit is comprised of *tiphkha* A and *tiphkha* B.

The benefit of using a tree-diagram is its clarity. Like diagramming a sentence in English, using a tree-diagram for the Hebrew accents shows you clearly what goes with what. One downside, however, is that this clarity can get lost as verses get longer and more complex. Another downside is that if you are working with a word processor, creating these trees is cumbersome. So, let's look at a second way to visualize the masoretic accents.

The only thing we're going to do is turn the tree-diagram on its side (or 90 degrees counterclockwise), so that the top becomes the left side of the visualization and the bottom becomes the right side.

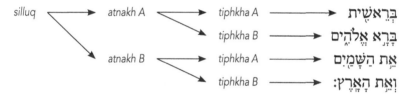

Start by looking at the right side of the diagram, and you will see that the verse is once again divided after each disjunctive accent: *tiphkha, atnakh, tiphkha,* and *silluq. Silluq* governs the whole verse and so is on the left side of the diagram. *Atnakh* divides the verse in half, and each half is then divided in half by *tiphkha*.

If you happen to use Logos Bible Software, you already have access to this latter visualization for every verse in the Bible. Logos has a simple interactive called "Hebrew Cantillations."[27] This is what Genesis 1:1 looks like in this interactive:[28]

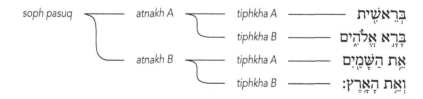

---

27. Logos Bible Software has a second interactive that gives a bit more detail and is called "Lexham Hebrew Bible: Cantillation Analysis Graph," which is supported by "Lexham Hebrew Bible: Cantillation Analysis Documentation."

28. Used with permission by the Faithlife Corporation, makers of Logos Bible Software—www.logos.com.

[Note that Logos is using *soph pasuq* for *silluq*.] This feature in Logos is interactive in that by placing your cursor on any label, for example *atnakh* A, you can easily see everything dominated by that label via highlighting:[29]

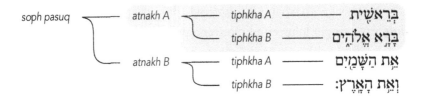

If you do not use Logos Bible Software, you can create this same kind of visualization on your own. Start by copying and pasting Genesis 1:1 into your document.

בְּרֵאשִׁ֖ית בָּרָ֣א אֱלֹהִ֑ים אֵ֥ת הַשָּׁמַ֖יִם וְאֵ֥ת הָאָֽרֶץ׃

Then place your cursor after the word containing *atnakh* and hit return.

בְּרֵאשִׁ֖ית בָּרָ֣א אֱלֹהִ֑ים
אֵ֥ת הַשָּׁמַ֖יִם וְאֵ֥ת הָאָֽרֶץ׃

Do the same for the remaining disjunctive accents.

בְּרֵאשִׁ֖ית
בָּרָ֣א אֱלֹהִ֑ים
אֵ֥ת הַשָּׁמַ֖יִם
וְאֵ֥ת הָאָֽרֶץ׃

You can now print out your diagram and add labels by hand or you can create a table with the appropriate number of rows and columns using one column for each set of labels and one column for each set of arrows. This takes a bit of time, but it ensures that you understand the syntactic relations

29. Used with permission by the Faithlife Corporation, makers of Logos Bible Software—www .logos.com.

in each verse according to the masoretic tradition by forcing you to slow down and read the text carefully.

A third and the easiest method of marking the units according to the masoretic accents is simply to copy and paste a verse into a word processing document and then add a series of lines to mark the divisions. Use one line to mark group 1 accents, two lines for group 2, three lines for group 3, and four lines for group 4.

בְּרֵאשִׁית // בָּרָא אֱלֹהִים / אֵת הַשָּׁמַיִם // וְאֵת הָאָרֶץ: /

Whether you choose to use Bible software or create visualizations on your own, the use of some kind of visualization is a great aid to seeing the relations of the parts of the text clearly.

1. So, when reading a verse with the masoretic accents, start by marking the group 1 accents: *silluq* and *atnakh*. Now you have your verse in two halves.
2. Next mark your group 2 accents: *segolta, zaqeph,* and *tiphkha.*
3. Then mark your group 3 accents: *revia, zarqa, pashta,* and *tevir.*
4. Finally, mark your group 4 accents: *pazer* and *geresh.*

PRACTICE READING WITH THE DISJUNCTIVE ACCENTS

Let's conclude this chapter with some practice by reading Genesis 1:2 and 1:3 with the masoretic accents.

Example #1: Genesis 1:2

וְהָאָרֶץ הָיְתָה תֹהוּ וָבֹהוּ וְחֹשֶׁךְ עַל־פְּנֵי תְהוֹם
וְרוּחַ אֱלֹהִים מְרַחֶפֶת עַל־פְּנֵי הַמָּיִם:

Now the earth was formless and empty,

darkness was over the surface of the deep,

and the spirit of God was hovering over the waters.

First, note the location of the group 1 accents: *silluq* on the final word הַמָּיִם and *atnakh* on תְהֹום. You now see the two halves of the verse. Second, note the location of the first strongest accent of the group 2 accents: *zaqeph* on וָבֹהוּ in verse 1a and *zaqeph* on אֱלֹהִים in verse 1b. You now see the halves of each half of the verse. Third, note the location of the second strongest accent of the group 2 accents: *tiphkha* on וְחֹשֶׁךְ in verse 1a and *tiphkha* on מְרַחֶפֶת in verse 1b. You can now see the halves of the halves of each half of the verse. Fourth, note the location of the first strongest accent in the group 3 accents: *revia* on וְהָאָרֶץ in verse 1a. Finally, note the location of the next strongest accent in the group 3 accents: *pashta* on תֹהוּ in verse 1a. The result can be visualized something like this:

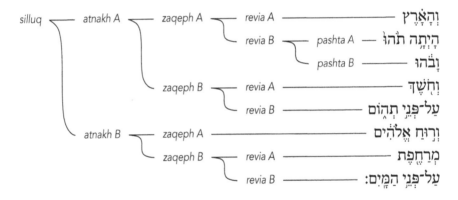

The first thing you might notice is that *atnakh* A contains two negative conditions ("formless and empty, darkness was over the surface of the deep") and *atnakh* B contains one positive condition ("and the spirit of God was hovering over the waters"). In the beginning, the earth was no place for human flourishing, but there was a harbinger of hope for better things to come.

The second thing you might notice is that "formless and empty" in *zaqeph* A needs to be separated from "darkness was over the deep" in *zaqeph* B. These two negative conditions, while related, need to be differentiated. God will take care of the "formless and empty" throughout the six days of creation, and he will begin by bounding the "darkness" on the first day.

The third thing you might notice is that "darkness" in *tiphkha* A is separated from "over the surface of the deep" in *tiphkha* B. This is something like placing "darkness" in a bold or italic font to draw it to your attention. Attention is drawn in a similar way to "the spirit of God" by separating it in *zaqeph* A from "was hovering over the waters" in *zaqeph* B.

The final thing you might notice is the isolation of "the earth" in *revia* A. This accent highlights the fronting of the subject, which shows us what is going to be the focus of the six days of creation—not the celestial realm of God and the angels, but the terrestrial realm of God's soon-to-be image bearers.

Example #2: Genesis 1:3

וַיֹּאמֶר אֱלֹהִים יְהִי אֹור וַיְהִי־אֹור׃

And God said, "Let there be light."

First, note the location of the group 1 accents: *silluq* on וַיְהִי־אֹור and *atnakh* on אֹור. You now see the two halves of the verse. Second, note the location of any accent in the group 2 accents: *zaqeph* on אֱלֹהִים in verse 1a. You now you see the halves of the first half of the verse. The result can be visualized something like this:

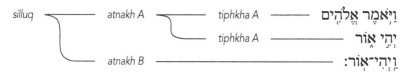

The first thing you might notice is the separation of God's speech in *atnakh* A from the result of that speech in *atnakh* B. In Genesis 1:1–2:3, the analog to וַיְהִי־אֹור is וַיְהִי־כֵן, which will always occur in such isolation in *atnakh* B on the remaining days of creation, highlighting in a rhythmic way the effectiveness of God's creative word.

The second thing you might notice is the separation of the introduction to divine speech in *tiphkha* A from the speech itself in *tiphkha* B. There is nothing profoundly theological here, but you will see this kind of separation routinely not only in Genesis 1:1–2:3 but throughout the Hebrew Bible.

Now that you are familiar with the disjunctive accents, it is time to meet the conjunctive accents in the following chapter.

CHAPTER 3

THE ACCENTS AND SENSE, PART TWO:

The Conjunctive Accents

This chapter on the conjunctive accents will be shorter than the previous chapter on the disjunctive accents and easier to master for three reasons: (1) there is only one group since the conjunctive accents all exhibit the same "power"—there is no hierarchy of strength,[1] (2) there are fewer of them, and (3) we are only going to focus on the four most frequent. In addition, there is evidence that the conjunctive accents were of secondary importance to the disjunctive accents. For example, in the Babylonian and Palestinian traditions conjunctive accents were not marked; only the disjunctives were indicated.[2] Before looking at how the conjunctive accents work, let's review their names and symbols.

REVIEW OF THE CONJUNCTIVE ACCENTS

Hebrew Name	English Name	Symbol	Symbol
מֵרְכָא	merekha	טֱטֱט	֖
מֵרְכָא כְּפוּלָה	merekha kephulah[3]	טֱטֱט	֑
מוּנָח	munakh	טֱטֱט	֣
מְהֻפָּ֤ח	mehuppakh	טֱטֱט	֤

(cont.)

---

1. Khan, *A Short Introduction*, 38.
2. Khan, *A Short Introduction*, 38.
3. *Merekha kephulah* is a rare disjunctive accent, occurring only thirteen times. *Merekha kephulah* always comes before *tiphkha* and always follows *darga*. So, we will leave it aside at this point (except in summaries).

Hebrew Name	English Name	Symbol	Symbol
דַּרְגָּא	darga[4]	טטט	◌ֶ
אַזְלָא	azla[5]	טטט	◌ֶ
תְּלִישָׁא קְטַנָּה	telisha qetannah[6]	טטטֿ	◌ֶֿ
גַּלְגַּל	galgal[7]	טטט	◌ֶ

In general, the conjunctive accents do what their name implies: they join a word to the following word. For example, they join a direct object marker to the direct object (אֵת הַשָּׁמַיִם; Gen 1:1), a noun that is in the construct state to the noun with which it is in construction (וְרוּחַ אֱלֹהִים; Gen 1:2), a verb to its subject (וַיֹּאמֶר אֱלֹהִים; Gen 1:3), or a preposition to the noun it governs (מִתַּחַת הַשָּׁמַיִם; Gen 1:9). Also, as with a construct chain of nouns, most of the time you will have two words joined by a conjunctive accent. But as you can have multiple nouns in a construct chain, you can also have multiple conjunctive accents before a disjunctive, for example, כִּי בוֹ שָׁבַת (munakh, mehuppakh, pashta; Gen 2:3) and וַיַּעַשׂ אֱלֹהִים אֶת־חַיַּת הָאָרֶץ (munakh, telisha qetannah, azla, geresh; Gen 1:25). In short, the conjunctive accents are placed on words in between the disjunctive accents, and they thereby show the words that are to be treated as a unit, starting with the first conjunctive accent and ending with a disjunctive accent.[8]

When we studied the disjunctive accents, we moved from the strongest to the weakest. In a similar way, let's study the conjunctive accents in descending order according to the power of the disjunctive accent that follows. First let's look at the conjunctive accents that precede the major disjunctive accents (group 1 and group 2), in particular *silluq*,[9] *atnakh*, and

---

4. *Darga* occurs 3,277 times. *Darga* most frequently comes before *tevir* but also on occasion before *revia* and rarely before *tiphcha* (fourteen times). We will leave it aside at this point (except in summaries).

5. An alternative name is *qadma* (קַדְמָא).

6. *Telisha qetannah* is a relatively rare disjunctive accent, occurring only 1,436 times. *Telisha qetannah* always precedes *geresh* but not immediately; there is always at least an *azla* in between. We will leave it aside at this point (except in summaries).

7. *Galgal* is a rare conjunctive accent, occurring only sixteen times. *Galgal* always comes before *pazer gadol*, which is itself relatively rare, occurring only sixteen times. So, we will leave it aside at this point (except in summaries).

8. Khan, *A Short Introduction*, 37.

9. In connection with *silluq*, we will look at *merekha* as it precedes *tiphkha*.

zaqeph, and then let's study those that precede a couple of minor disjunctive accents (group 3 and group 4), in particular *revia*, *zarqa*, *pashta*, and *geresh*.

USE OF THE CONJUNCTIVE ACCENTS WITH THE MAJOR DISJUNCTIVE ACCENTS

Merekha ֵ

Merekha ֵ is the conjunctive accent that will occur immediately before *silluq*, the strongest disjunctive accent (when *silluq* is not preceded by a disjunctive accent).

Example #1: Genesis 1:1

אֵת הַשָּׁמַיִם וְאֵת הָאָרֶץ:	בְּרֵאשִׁית בָּרָא אֱלֹהִים
the heavens and the earth	In the beginning God created

Example #2: Genesis 1:2b

מְרַחֶפֶת עַל־פְּנֵי הַמָּיִם:	וְרוּחַ אֱלֹהִים
was hovering over the waters.	And the spirit of God

If *silluq* is preceded by a disjunctive accent, that accent will be *tiphkha*, and if this *tiphkha* is preceded by a conjunctive accent, it will be *merekha*.

Example #3: Genesis 1:6b

בֵּין מַיִם לָמָיִם:	וִיהִי מַבְדִּיל
between water to water	And let it be separating

Example #4: Genesis 2:3b

אֲשֶׁר־בָּרָא אֱלֹהִים לַעֲשׂוֹת:	כִּי בוֹ שָׁבַת מִכָּל־מְלַאכְתּוֹ
which God created to do	because on it he rested from all his work

Note: *merekha* will frequently precede *tiphkha* in other environments as well.

Example #5: Genesis 1:3a

יְהִי אֽוֹר	וַיֹּ֥אמֶר אֱלֹהִ֖ים
"Let there be light."	And God said,

Example #6: Genesis 1:6a

יְהִי רָקִ֙יעַ֙ בְּת֣וֹךְ הַמָּ֑יִם	וַיֹּ֣אמֶר אֱלֹהִ֗ים
"Let there be a vault between the waters."	And God said,

The main thing to keep in mind is that you will routinely see *merekha* before *silluq*, the strongest disjunctive accent. You will also see *merekha* before *tiphkha*, whether that *tiphkha* is before *silluq* or elsewhere.[10]

Munakh ◌֣

Munakh ◌֣, the most frequent conjunctive accent, is the conjunctive accent that will occur immediately before *atnakh*, the second strongest disjunctive accent (when *atnakh* is not preceded by a disjunctive accent).

Example #1: Genesis 1:1a

בָּרָ֣א אֱלֹהִ֑ים	בְּרֵאשִׁ֖ית
God created	In the beginning

Example #2: Genesis 1:3a

יְהִי אֽוֹר	וַיֹּ֣אמֶר אֱלֹהִ֑ים
"Let there be light."	And God said,

Munakh is also the conjunctive accent that will occur immediately before *zaqeph*, the third-strongest disjunctive accent (when *zaqeph* is not preceded by a disjunctive accent).

---

10. *Merekha* occurs elsewhere, but keep in mind that this is an introduction to the accents, not an exhaustive treatment.

Example #3: Genesis 1:2b

וְר֣וּחַ אֱלֹהִ֔ים	מְרַחֶ֖פֶת עַל־פְּנֵ֥י הַמָּֽיִם׃
and the spirit of God	was hovering over the waters.

Example #4: Genesis 1:16

וַיַּ֣עַשׂ אֱלֹהִ֔ים	אֶת־שְׁנֵ֥י הַמְּאֹרֹ֖ת הַגְּדֹלִ֑ים
God made	the two great lights

The main thing to keep in mind is that you will routinely see *munakh* before *atnakh*, the second-strongest disjunctive accent. You will also see *munakh* before *zaqeph*, the third-strongest disjunctive accent.[11]

USE OF THE CONJUNCTIVE ACCENTS WITH THE MINOR DISJUNCTIVE ACCENTS

Munakh ◌

Munakh ◌ is the conjunctive accent that will occur immediately before *revia*, a group 3 disjunctive accent.

Example #1: Genesis 1:11

וַיֹּ֣אמֶר אֱלֹהִ֔ים	תַּֽדְשֵׁ֤א הָאָ֨רֶץ֙ דֶּ֔שֶׁא
And God said,	"Let the land produce vegetation."

Example #2: Genesis 1:29

הִנֵּה֩ נָתַ֨תִּי לָכֶ֜ם	אֶת־כָּל־עֵ֣שֶׂב ׀ זֹרֵ֣עַ זֶ֗רַע
I give you	every plant bearing seed

Munakh ◌ is also the conjunctive accent that will occur immediately before *zarqa*, another group 3 disjunctive accent.

---

11. *Munakh* occurs elsewhere (see below), but keep in mind that this is an introduction to the accents, not an exhaustive treatment.

Example #3: Genesis 1:7

אֶת־הָרָקִיעַ	וַיַּעַשׂ אֱלֹהִים
the vault	So God made

Example #4: Genesis 1:28

אֱלֹהִים	וַיְבָרֶךְ אֹתָם
God	And blessed them

Mehuppakh ◌

Mehuppakh ◌ is the conjunctive accent that will occur immediately before *pashta*, a group 3 disjunctive accent.[12]

Example #1: Genesis 1:11

עֹשֶׂה פְּרִי	עֵץ פְּרִי
producing fruit	fruit trees

Example #2: Genesis 1:14

יְהִי מְאֹרֹת	וַיֹּאמֶר אֱלֹהִים
"Let there be lights"	And God said,

Azla ◌

Azla ◌ is the conjunctive accent that will occur immediately before *geresh*, a group 4 disjunctive accent.

Example #1: Genesis 1:24

נֶפֶשׁ חַיָּה	תּוֹצֵא הָאָרֶץ
living creatures	Let the land produce

---

12. Remember that *mehuppakh* looks like *yetiv*, but *yetiv* is prepositive. Compare בְּי (*yetiv* in Gen 3:5) and בְּי (*mehuppakh* in Gen 4:12).

Example #2: Genesis 1:25

אֶת־חַיַּת הָאָ֫רֶץ	וַיַּ֫עַשׂ אֱלֹהִים֙
the wild animals	God made

SUMMARY OF THE CONJUNCTIVE ACCENTS

Memorize these four conjunctive accents in the following order, which descends according to the strength of the disjunctive accent that follows. And memorize the pairs of conjunctive/disjunctive accents, for example, *merekha/silluq*, *merekha/tiphkha*, *munakh/atnakh*, etc. With this memorization, you will be familiar with the lion's share of the conjunctive accents in your Hebrew Bible.

Accent	Group 1	Group 2	Group 3	Group 4
merekha	silluq	tiphkha		
munakh	atnakh	zaqeph	revia zarqa	
mehuppakh			pashta	
azla				geresh

PRACTICE READING WITH THE CONJUNCTIVE
AND DISJUNCTIVE ACCENTS

Let's conclude this chapter by looking at one verse that will help us put the conjunctive and disjunctive accents together, Genesis 17:1.

וַיְהִ֣י אַבְרָ֔ם בֶּן־תִּשְׁעִ֥ים שָׁנָ֖ה וְתֵ֣שַׁע שָׁנִ֑ים

וַיֵּרָ֨א יְהֹוָ֜ה אֶל־אַבְרָ֗ם וַיֹּ֤אמֶר אֵלָיו֙ אֲנִי־אֵ֣ל שַׁדַּ֔י

הִתְהַלֵּ֥ךְ לְפָנַ֖י וֶהְיֵ֥ה תָמִֽים:

When Abram was ninety-nine years old,

the Lord appeared to him and said, "I am God Almighty;

walk before me faithfully and be blameless."

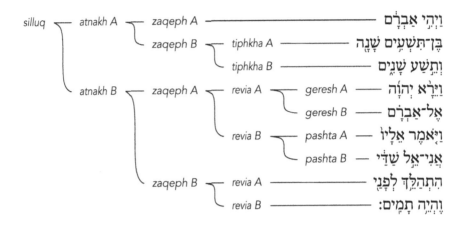

This verse is divided in half by *atnakh* (שָׁנִים), which separates the background information (v. 1a) from the Lord's appearance to Abram (v. 1b). The first half is divided in half by *zaqeph* (אַבְרָם), which separates the predicate and subject (v. 1aα[13]) from the subject complement (v. 1aβ). The second half is also divided by *zaqeph* (שַׁדָּי), which separates the Lord's revelation of himself (v. 1bα) from his command to Abram (v. 1bβ).

The conjunctive accents occur where you would expect them based on our previous discussion. First, merekha occurs right before silluq at the end of the verse (וְהְיֵה תָמִים). Second, munakh occurs right before atnakh at the midpoint of the verse (וְתֵשַׁע שָׁנִים). Third, munakh also occurs before zaqeph twice (וַיְהִי אַבְרָם and אֲנִי־אֵל שַׁדָּי). Fourth, mehuppakh occurs before pashta (וַיֹּאמֶר אֵלָיו). Fifth, merekha occurs before tiphkha twice (בֶּן־תִּשְׁעִים שָׁנָה and הִתְהַלֵּךְ לְפָנַי). And sixth, azla occurs before geresh (וַיֵּרָא יְהוָה).

Now that we have the basics of both the disjunctive and conjunctive accents down, we can turn our attention in the next chapter to examining a number of texts where reading with the accents makes a difference exegetically, sometimes minor and sometimes major.

---

13. It is traditional to use Greek letters to refer to the halves of half verses, so verse 1aα refers to the first half of the first half of verse 1.

CHAPTER 4

THE ACCENTS
AND EXEGESIS

Students who know Hebrew are often looking for commentaries to help them deal with the exegetical details of the Hebrew text. They need look no further than their Masoretic Text, which provides a detailed exegetical analysis of the text by means of the accents. Now the accents will not help with all matters exegetical, but they do provide an ancient commentary on the syntactic relations of every word in every verse of the Hebrew Bible.

Frequently enough, there is nothing all that exciting that comes to light exegetically from paying attention to the accents. But there are plenty of cases where paying attention to the accents affects one's understanding of the text. Sometimes these differences are subtle, though subtle does not mean unimportant. At other times the accents make a major difference in our understanding of the text—I should say, in our understanding of the ancient Masoretes' understanding of the text. And it needs to be said that sometimes at our distance from the Masoretes we have a hard time understanding what they were thinking and why they accented the text as they did.[1]

In this chapter we're going to do some focused exegetical work through the lens of the masoretic accents. First, we will look at some texts where the accents make a subtle difference in our interpretation. Second, we will look at some texts where the accents make a more significant difference. Third, we will look at a couple of texts where it appears that there are errors in the masoretic placement of the accents.

---

1. Yeivin, *Introduction to the Tiberian Masorah*, 171.

SUBTLE DIFFERENCES

There is no place to start like the beginning, so let's look at Genesis 1:1.

Example #1: Genesis 1:1

בְּרֵאשִׁית בָּרָא אֱלֹהִים אֵת הַשָּׁמַיִם וְאֵת הָאָרֶץ:

In the beginning God created the heavens and the earth.

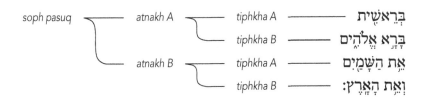

Silluq (הָאָרֶץ) marks the end of the verse, and *atnakh* (אֱלֹהִים) marks the midpoint, separating the predicate and the subject (*atnakh* A) from the direct objects (*atnakh* B). *Tiphcha* (הַשָּׁמַיִם) divides the second half of the verse in half, separating the two components of the direct object. *Tiphcha* (בְּרֵאשִׁית) also divides the first half of the verse in half, separating the temporal phrase from the predicate and subject. *Munakh* (בָּרָא) is the expected conjunctive accent before *atnakh*, and *merekha* (וְאֵת and אֵת) is the expected conjunctive accent before *silluq* and *tiphcha*, respectively.

From a grammatical point of view, *atnakh* separates the subject and the predicate from the direct objects. But why not place *atnakh* on the temporal phrase (בְּרֵאשִׁית) and separate this phrase from the predicate, subject, and direct objects? The answer is that from a rhetorical point of view *atnakh* is emphasizing the word אֱלֹהִים. Wickes provides numerous examples of the use of *atnakh* to focus on or emphasize a component of a verse.[2] Here the focus is not on the fact that God created "in the beginning," or that God "created," but that "God" (and no other) created.[3] So when contemporary Bible scholars tell us that Genesis 1:1 is a polemic against the religions of the surrounding cultures, they are simply reiterating what the accents told us long ago through the placement of *atnakh*.

---

2. Wickes, *A Treatise on the Twenty-One*, 32.
3. See Fuller and Choi, *Hebrew Syntax*, 384.

Now it might strike one as odd to think of *atnakh* being placed on the first word of a verse, but this happens fifty-three times in the Hebrew Bible.[4] See for example Ezekiel 34:19.

וְצֹאנִי מִרְמַס רַגְלֵיכֶם תִּרְעֶינָה
וּמִרְפַּשׂ רַגְלֵיכֶם תִּשְׁתֶּינָה

My flock—must it feed on what you have trampled
and drink what you have muddied with your feet?

Why not place *atnakh* on תִּרְעֶינָה ("must it feed"), separating the "feeding" clause from the "drinking" clause? Because the focus is on וְצֹאנִי, God's own personal flock.

A related example is Genesis 6:8.

וְנֹחַ מָצָא חֵן בְּעֵינֵי יְהוָה:

But Noah found favor in the eyes of the LORD.

Zaqeph gadol (וְנֹחַ) is the disjunctive accent that divides this short verse in half and focuses on *Noah* as the object of the Lord's favor, as opposed to those involved in the wicked activity of verses 1–7.

Example #2: Genesis 1:11
וַיֹּאמֶר אֱלֹהִים תַּדְשֵׁא הָאָרֶץ דֶּשֶׁא
עֵשֶׂב מַזְרִיעַ זֶרַע עֵץ פְּרִי עֹשֶׂה פְּרִי לְמִינוֹ
אֲשֶׁר זַרְעוֹ־בוֹ
עַל־הָאָרֶץ וַיְהִי־כֵן:

Then God said, "Let the land produce vegetation:
seed-bearing plants and trees on the land that bear fruit with seed in it,
according to their various kinds."
And it was so. (NIV)

---

4. James D. Price, *The Syntax of Masoretic Accents in the Hebrew Bible: Studies in the Bible and Early Christianity* (New York: Mellen, 1990), 1.53.

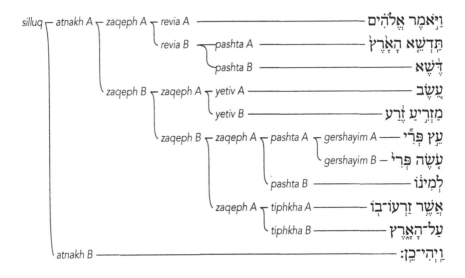

Atnakh (עַל־הָאָרֶץ) divides the verse in half, separating God's action of creating the vegetation (*atnakh* A) from the summary statement (*atnakh* B). *Zaqeph* divides the first half in half, separating the general (*zaqeph* A) from the specific (*zaqeph* B). The verse says that God created vegetation (דֶּשֶׁא) and that this vegetation is of two kinds, "seed-bearing plants" and "trees on the land that bear fruit with seed in it, according to their various kinds." Note the clarity of the NIV at this point, as it places a semicolon after "vegetation," whereas the ESV obscures the logic of the verse by placing a comma after "vegetation."

Example #3: Genesis 1:24

וַיֹּאמֶר אֱלֹהִים
תּוֹצֵא הָאָרֶץ נֶפֶשׁ חַיָּה לְמִינָהּ
בְּהֵמָה וָרֶמֶשׂ
וְחַיְתוֹ־אֶרֶץ לְמִינָהּ
וַיְהִי־כֵן:

And God said,

"Let the land produce living creatures according to their kinds:

the livestock, the creatures that move along the ground,

and the wild animals, each according to its kind."

And it was so. (NIV)

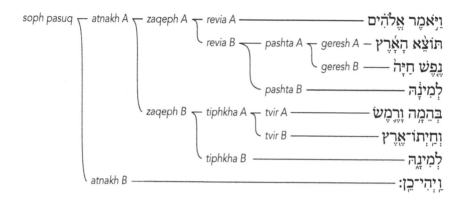

Atnakh (לְמִינָהּ) divides the verse in half, separating God's action of creating the animals (*atnakh* A) from the summary statement (*atnakh* B). *Zaqeph* divides the first half in half, separating the general (*zaqeph* A) from the specific (*zaqeph* B). The verse says that God created animals according to their kinds (נֶפֶשׁ חַיָּה לְמִינָהּ) and that these animals can be batched into two kinds, בְּהֵמָה and וָרֶמֶשׂ on the one hand (note the *merekha* on בְּהֵמָה) and וְחַיְתוֹ־אֶרֶץ לְמִינָהּ on the other. Note the clarity of the NIV at this point, as it places a semicolon after "living creatures according to their kinds," and note how the ESV accomplishes the same with its use of an em dash.

Example #4: Genesis 10:21

וּלְשֵׁם יֻלַּד גַּם־הֽוּא
אֲבִי כָּל־בְּנֵי־עֵבֶר אֲחִי יֶפֶת הַגָּדֽוֹל׃

And to Shem also sons were born—
the ancestor of all the sons of Eber, the big brother of Japheth.

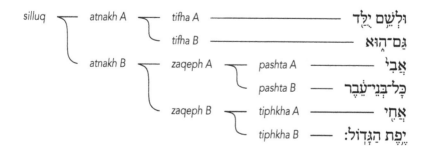

Atnakh (גַּם־הוּא) divides the verse in half, separating the main predication (*atnakh* A) from two appositional qualifiers (*atnakh* B). *Zaqeph* (כָּל־בְּנֵי־עֵבֶר) divides the second half of the verse in half, separating the two qualifiers. But is Shem the older brother of Japheth or is Japheth the older brother of Shem? The NIV opts for the latter and provides the alternative in a footnote.

> Sons were also born to Shem, whose older brother was Japheth; Shem was the ancestor of all the sons of Eber. (NIV)

The NLT, ESV, and the NJPS opt for the former with the NLT and ESV providing the alternative in a footnote.

> Sons were also born to Shem, the older brother of Japheth. Shem was the ancestor of all the descendants of Eber. (NLT)

> To Shem also, the father of all the children of Eber, the elder brother of Japheth, children were born. (ESV)

> Sons were also born to Shem, ancestor of all the descendants of Eber and older brother of Japheth. (NJPS)

The grammar and the accents favor the interpretation that Shem is the older brother of Japheth. To understand יֶפֶת הַגָּדוֹל as "Japheth the elder," i.e., the older brother, is ungrammatical, since proper nouns cannot be qualified by an adjective.[5] The adjective in this case (הַגָּדוֹל) would qualify the first noun in the construct chain (אֲחִי), hence "the big brother of Japheth." And the fact that אֲבִי כָּל־בְּנֵי־עֵבֶר and אֲחִי יֶפֶת הַגָּדוֹל are coordinate units in appositional relationship separated by *zaqeph* in verse 21b favors the interpretation that both have the same function as qualifiers of verse 21a; Shem is "the ancestor of all the sons of Eber" and "the big/older brother of Japheth."[6]

---

5. Joüon §141c and *BHRG* §30.2.2.7.
6. This interpretation also accords with the order of the names in Gen 5:32 and 6:10, "Shem, Ham, and Japheth."

Example #5: Genesis 12:3

וַאֲבָרְכָה מְבָרְכֶ֔יךָ
וּמְקַלֶּלְךָ֖ אָאֹ֑ר
וְנִבְרְכוּ בְךָ֔ כֹּ֖ל מִשְׁפְּחֹ֥ת הָאֲדָמָֽה׃

I will bless those who bless you,

and whoever curses you I will curse;

and all peoples on earth will be blessed through you. (NIV)

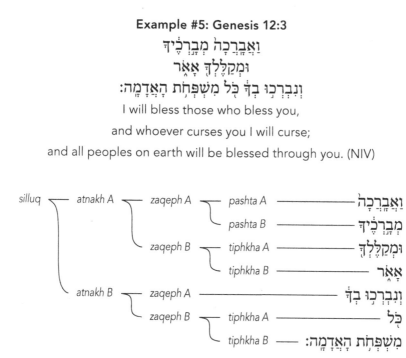

By its use of commas, the ESV leads the reader to divide this verse in thirds:

I will bless those who bless you,
    and him who dishonors you I will curse,
    and in you all the families of the earth shall be blessed.

But the *atnakh* (אָאֹ֑ר) divides the verse in two, separating God's actions (*atnakh* A) from the results of those actions (*atnakh* B). The NIV captures this somewhat by its use of a semicolon after "curse." The NLT captures the flow of thought even better with its use of a period:

I will bless those who bless you and curse those who treat you with contempt.
    All the families on earth will be blessed through you.

Example #6: Deuteronomy 6:7

וְשִׁנַּנְתָּם לְבָנֶיךָ וְדִבַּרְתָּ בָּם
בְּשִׁבְתְּךָ בְּבֵיתֶךָ וּבְלֶכְתְּךָ בַדֶּרֶךְ
וּבְשָׁכְבְּךָ וּבְקוּמֶךָ׃

Repeat[7] them to your children by talking[8] about them
when you sit in your house and when you walk along the road
and when you lie down and when you get up.

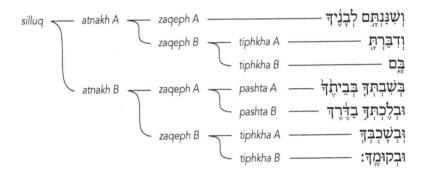

Atnakh (בָּם) divides this verse in half, separating the command (*atnakh* A) from the four qualifiers (*atnakh* B). *Zaqeph* (לְבָנֶיךָ) divides the first half in half, separating the two verbs that form one command ("Repeat . . . by speaking"). *Zaqeph* (בַדֶּרֶךְ) also divides the second half of the verse in half, separating the four qualifiers into two groups, each containing a pair: "sit in your house" and "walk along the road" (*zaqeph* A) and "lie down" and "get up" (*zaqeph* B). These pairs form merisms for "everywhere" and "all the time."

Owing to the separation of verse 7a from verse 7b by *atnakh*, the four qualifiers in verse 7b modify the whole of verse 7a ("Repeat them to your children by talking about them") and not just verse 7aβ ("by talking about them"), a nuance missed by all major translations. The NRSV comes the closest to capturing the flow of thought but would be improved with the addition of a comma after the second "them":

---

7. The precise meaning of the *piel* of שׁנן is debated. In my opinion the best interpretation is to take it from II שׁנן "to repeat" and not from I שׁנן "to sharpen." The root II שׁנן could be a by-form of II שׁנה "to repeat" (*HALOT* 4.1606), or it could be a denominative from שֵׁנִי "second." That being said, my analysis of the text in terms of the significance of the accents for the flow of thought does not depend upon the correctness of this interpretation.

8. I would take the underlying Hebrew verb form as epexegetical/explanatory; see Joüon §118j and *BHRG* §21.2.1.2.2.

Recite them to your children and talk about them when you are at home and when you are away, when you lie down and when you rise. (NRSV)

In linguistic terms *silluq* (וּבְקוּמֶךָ) dominates both *atnakh* A and *atnakh* B and so is called the "mother." *Atnakh* A and *atnakh* B are called "daughters," since they are both dominated by the same "mother."

There is a simple rule for daughter association: any daughter phrase may be directly associated only with the complete set of daughter phrases which are also dominated by its mother.[9]

In other words, *atnakh* B qualifies the whole of *atnakh* A. Parents are to teach their children by repeatedly speaking of the commandments everywhere and all the time.

Example #7: Job 42:11aα

וַיָּבֹאוּ אֵלָיו כָּל־אֶחָיו וְכָל־אַחְיֹתָיו
וְכָל־יֹדְעָיו לְפָנִים
וַיֹּאכְלוּ עִמּוֹ לֶחֶם בְּבֵיתוֹ

Then came to him all his brothers and sisters
and all who had known him before,
and ate bread with him in his house. (ESV)

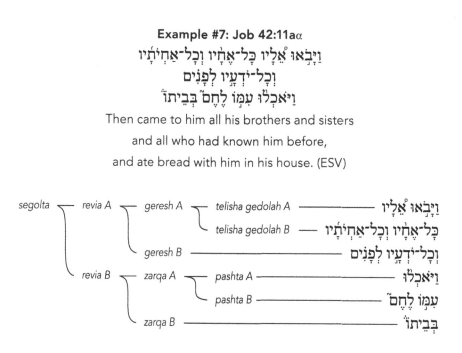

---

9. Robinson and Levy, "The Masoretes and the Punctuation of Biblical Hebrew," 18.

The word order of the ESV is not felicitous, but it captures the sense of the text at one point in particular. The ESV makes clear that there are two groups that came to Job: "his brothers and sisters" and "all who had known him before." The NIV ("All his brothers and sisters and everyone who had known him before") is ambiguous, and the NLT ("Then all his brothers, sisters, and former friends came") ignores the accents altogether.

Segolta (בְּבֵיתוֹ) marks the end of the first half of the first half of the verse. *Revia* (לְפָנִים) divides the *segolta* unit in half, separating the two main clauses. *Telisha gedolah* (אֵלָיו) divides *revia* A in half, separating the predicate and indirect object from the subjects. *Geresh* (וְכָל־אַחְיֹתָיו) separates the first subject ("all his brothers and sisters") from the second subject ("and all who had known him before"). That "all his brothers and sisters" serves as one subject is confirmed by the conjunctive *azla* (כָּל־אֶחָיו וְכָל־אַחְיֹתָיו). So, there are not three groups that came to Job but two: "all his brothers and sisters" and "all who had known him before."

SIGNIFICANT DIFFERENCES

Having looked at examples of subtle differences, we can now look at examples where reading with the accents is more significant for exegesis.[10]

Example #1: Genesis 1:21

וַיִּבְרָא אֱלֹהִים אֶת־הַתַּנִּינִם הַגְּדֹלִים
וְאֵת כָּל־נֶפֶשׁ הַחַיָּה׀ הָרֹמֶשֶׂת אֲשֶׁר שָׁרְצוּ הַמַּיִם
לְמִינֵהֶם וְאֵת כָּל־עוֹף כָּנָף לְמִינֵהוּ
וַיַּרְא אֱלֹהִים כִּי־טוֹב׃

So God created the great sea monsters,
and every living creature which moves with which the water teems
according to their kinds, and every winged bird according to its kind.
And God saw that it was good.

---

10. Of course, the boundary between subtle and significant is fuzzy and subjective, but it has a heuristic value.

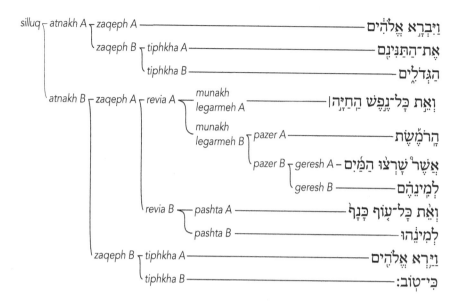

Atnakh (הַגְּדֹלִֽים) divides the verse in half, oddly separating the predicate, subject, and first direct object ("So God created the great sea monsters") from two other direct objects ("and every living creature which moves with which the water teems according to their kinds, and every winged bird according to its kind") and the entire second main clause ("And God saw that it was good"). *Zaqeph* (לְמִינֵ֑הוּ) divides the second half of the verse in half, separating the two direct objects that belong to the first clause ("every living creature which moves with which the water teems according to their kinds, and every winged bird according to its kind") from the second main clause ("And God saw that it was good"). What might the Masoretes have been thinking or, better, what is the interpretation of this verse that the Masoretes have encoded?

First, note that "there was evening and there was morning" occupies *atnakh* B on days 1, 2, and 6 (vv. 5, 8, 31) and that this clause is a separate verse altogether on days 3, 4, and 5 (verses 13, 19, 23). Note also that the predication of טוֹב ("good") is at the end of *atnakh* A on days 1 and 6 (vv. 4 and 31) and at the end of *atnakh* B on days 2, 3, 4, and 5 (vv. 10, 12, 18, 21). These two phenomena show that while there is a high level of regularity in Genesis 1:1–2:3 that regularity is not rigid. Perhaps these differences are important for the interpretation of the text. The point is that these differences prompt us to wonder whether or not the placing of *atnakh* at the end of אֶת־הַתַּנִּינִם הַגְּדֹלִים ("the great sea monsters") rather than on לְמִינֵהוּ ("according to its kind"), which seems to be the logical place to put *atnakh* and would result in a neat division of the verse into two clauses ("So God created the great sea monsters . . . And God saw that it was good"), is significant for the interpretation of this verse.

Second, the use of the word הַתַּנִּינִם ("sea monsters") strikes an ominous cord. Sometimes the word תַּנִּין refers to ordinary snakes, but even when it does there are ominous overtones (see Exod 7:9 and Jer 51:34). Then there are texts where תַּנִּין refers to the king of Egypt as a great adversary of God and his kingdom (see Ezek 29:3 and 32:2). Finally there are texts where תַּנִּין is used as an analog to Leviathan (Isa 27:1 and Ps 74:13), the opponent of God. Note also that as in in Genesis 1:21 so in Psalm 74:13 the plural is used (שִׁבַּרְתָּ רָאשֵׁי תַנִּינִים), which the NIV renders as a singular for a multiheaded monster: "you broke the heads of the monster."

Third, in verse 21b the *zaqeph* A and *zaqeph* B units are dominated by *atnakh*. Given the daughter relationship, *zaqeph* B ("And God saw that it was good") only qualifies *zaqeph* A ("and every living creature which moves with which the water teems according to their kinds, and every winged bird according to its kind"). *Atnakh* placed on הַתַּנִּינִם הַגְּדֹלִים ("the great sea monsters") dissociates הַתַּנִּינִם הַגְּדֹלִים from "And God saw that it was good." If the *atnakh* had been placed at the end of the first clause, then "And God saw that it was good" (*atnakh* B) would qualify the entire first half of the verse (*atnakh* A), including, "So God created the great sea monsters," since *atnakh* A and *atnakh* B would be daughters of *silluq*.

> In the masoretic punctuation the daughter association of "and God saw that it was good" only extends backward to nodes under the second *zaqeph*, thus avoiding the implication that the sea-monsters were good![11]

---

11. Robinson and Levy, "The Masoretes and the Punctuation of Biblical Hebrew," 20.

One may or may not agree with this interpretation, but this surely seems to be the interpretation encoded in the accents by the Masoretes.[12]

Example #2: Genesis 6:4

הַנְּפִלִים הָיָוּ בָאָרֶץ בַּיָּמִים הָהֵם

וְגַם אַחֲרֵי־כֵן אֲשֶׁר יָבֹאוּ בְּנֵי הָאֱלֹהִים אֶל־בְּנוֹת הָאָדָם

וְיָלְדוּ לָהֶם

הֵמָּה הַגִּבֹּרִים אֲשֶׁר מֵעוֹלָם אַנְשֵׁי הַשֵּׁם:

The Nephilim were in the land in those days

—and also afterward when the sons of God went to the daughters of humans

and had children by them—

They were the mighty warriors of old, men of renown.

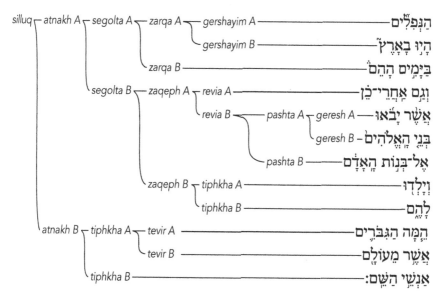

In the Hebrew Bible parenthetical material can be indicated in a variety of ways.[13] Take Genesis 19:20 as an example,

---

12. It can be pointed out that if this interpretation is correct, the "great sea monsters" are ultimately good, as they come under the umbrella of verse 31a, "God saw all that he had made, and it was very good."

13. WO §§30.5.2b, 32.3e, 39.2.3c.

הִנֵּה־נָ֠א הָעִ֨יר הַזֹּ֥את קְרֹבָ֛ה לָנ֥וּס שָׁ֖מָּה וְהִ֣יא מִצְעָ֑ר
אִמָּֽלְטָ֨ה נָּ֜א שָׁ֗מָּה הֲלֹ֥א מִצְעָ֛ר הִ֖וא וּתְחִ֥י נַפְשִֽׁי׃

Look, this city is near enough to run there; and it is small.

Let me flee there—isn't it small?—so that my life will be spared.

There is a general rule for how accents serve to reinforce the presence
of parenthetical material in the middle or at the end of a verse: "the rule is
to mark it off with the accent *next greater than that which precedes it.*"[14] So,
for example, a parenthesis that begins after *atnakh* continues until *silluq*,
and a parenthesis that begins after *zaqeph* continues until *atnakh* or *silluq*,
depending on which half of the verse contains the parenthesis.[15] You can
see this rule operating in Genesis 19:20, where the parenthesis begins after
revia (שָׁ֖מָּה) and ends at *tiphkha* (הִ֖וא).

The NIV and the NRSV are in agreement that there is a parenthesis in
Genesis 6:4. They take the parenthesis to be "and also afterward," marking
it out with an em dash. According to this reading, the sense of the text is,
"The Nephilim were in the land in those days . . . when the sons of God went
to the daughters of humans and had children by them." So, the temporal
reference to the cohabitation in this verse is the same as that in verse 2, the
antediluvian period. But starting the parenthesis after *segolta* (הָהֵ֒ם֒) and
ending at *revia* (אַחֲרֵי־כֵ֗ן) does not follow the general rule for accents and
parenthetical material. According to the rule, if the parenthesis starts after
segolta (הָהֵ֒ם֒), it should end at *atnakh* (לָהֶ֑ם), "the next greater." The NIV and
the NRSV are correct in discerning parenthetical material in this verse, but
the parenthesis is somewhat longer than they indicate: "—and also afterward
when the sons of God went to the daughters of humans and had children
by them—." The parenthesis informs us that the cohabitation of the sons
of God and daughters of humans referred to in verse 2 was not restricted to
the days before the flood but also occurred continuously[16] after the flood.

Marking out the parenthesis according to the accents has the benefit

---

14. Wickes, *A Treatise on the Twenty-One*, 42.

15. For a detailed discussion of the relationship between parenthetical material in the accents see
Fuller and Choi, *Hebrew Syntax*, 389–92.

16. The use of the imperfect (יָבֹ֣אוּ) followed by a *waw* relative perfect (וְיָלְד֖וּ) in a past time frame
is typical for continuous action in the past (*BHRG* §§19.3.4, 21.3.2).

of providing the easiest explanation for the presence of Nephilim after the flood, as evidenced in Numbers 13:33,

> We saw the Nephilim there (the descendants of Anak come from the Nephilim). We seemed like grasshoppers in our own eyes, and we looked the same to them. (NIV)

The cohabitation of the sons of God and the daughters of humans took place both before and after the flood, thus explaining the presence of their progeny, the Nephilim, both before and after the flood.

Example #3: Deuteronomy 26:5a

וְעָנִ֨יתָ וְאָמַרְתָּ֜ לִפְנֵ֣י ׀ יְהוָ֣ה אֱלֹהֶ֗יךָ
אֲרַמִּי֙ אֹבֵ֣ד אָבִ֔י
וַיֵּ֣רֶד מִצְרַ֔יְמָה וַיָּ֥גָר שָׁ֖ם בִּמְתֵ֥י מְעָֽט

You shall answer and say before the LORD your God,
"An Aramaean was pursuing my father,
so he went down to Egypt and lived there with a few people."

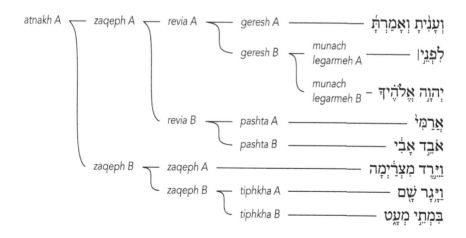

Modern translations render אֲרַמִּי֙ אֹבֵ֣ד אָבִ֔י with something like, "My father was a wandering Aramaean," but this is not the reading of the text provided by the Masoretes.

When the participle אֹבֵד is functioning as an attributive to a previous noun, as would be the case in "wandering Aramaean," the accent on that noun is conjunctive. For example, Psalm 31:13b[12b] (הָיִיתִי כִּכְלִי אֹבֵד ["I have become like broken pottery"]) has the conjunctive accent *mer-ekha* (כִּכְלִי) joining the noun to the following attributive participle (אֹבֵד). Another example is Psalm 119:176a (תָּעִיתִי כְּשֶׂה אֹבֵד בַּקֵּשׁ עַבְדֶּךָ, "I have strayed like a lost sheep"), which has the conjunctive accent *munakh* (כְּשֶׂה) joining the noun to the following attributive participle (אֹבֵד). So, we would expect a conjunctive accent on אֲרַמִּי if the Masoretes intended אֲרַמִּי אֹבֵד to mean "a wandering Aramaean."

Job 4:11a provides an analog to Deuteronomy 26:5, having a noun with a disjunctive accent followed by אֹבֵד as a predicate participle: לַיִשׁ אֹבֵד מִבְּלִי־טָרֶף ("The lion perishes for lack of prey"). So, the disjunctive accent on אֲרַמִּי in Deuteronomy 26:5 leads us to conclude that אֲרַמִּי is the subject of the predicate אֹבֵד, as is the case in Job 4:11a.

This understanding can be found in the Passover Haggadah.[17]

This verse is deployed in the Passover Haggadah (just following the section on the Four Sons) in a famous passage that emphasizes God's miraculous sparing of Israel from a long line of persecutors, beginning with Laban's attack on Jacob (Gen. ch 31). By means of a midrashic reworking of its original meaning, the verse is interpreted to mean "an Aramean sought to destroy my ancestor." That rendering departs from the actual grammar of the verse and almost certainly reflects the politics of the Second Temple period, when the Seleucid empire, which ruled Israel from Syria (198–168 BCE), was referred to obliquely as Laban, the Aramean. The hyperbolic claim in the Haggadah that Laban's oppression of Israel/Jacob was more invidious than the Egyptian enslavement points to a polemic against the Seleucids, whose policies triggered the Hasmonean revolt (167 BCE).[18]

---

17. Khan, *A Short Introduction*, 39.
18. Adele Berlin, Marc Zvi Brettler, and Michael A. Fishbane, eds., *The Jewish Study Bible: Jewish Publication Society Tanakh Translation* (Oxford: Oxford University Press, 2004), 423–24.

I am not sure why this comment refers to a midrashic reworking or says that it is ungrammatical to read אֲרַמִּי אֹבֵד אָבִי as "an Aramean sought to destroy my ancestor." Without the accents this reading is grammatically possible and with the accents it is almost certain. It seems to me that the Passover Haggadah is simply reflecting the same tradition as found in the masoretic accents. Moreover, referring to Jacob as an Aramaean would be odd, to say the least, in light of the way Aramaean is used elsewhere in a pejorative sense to distinguish the family of Abraham from the Aramaeans.[19]

The interpretation encoded in the Masoretic Text is also found in the Latin Vulgate, which reads, *Syrus persequebatur patrem meum*. *Syrus* ("A Syrian") is the subject, *persequebatur*[20] ("was pursuing/hunting out/attacking") is the predicate, and *patrem meum* ("my father") is the direct object. So the Vulgate can be translated, "A Syrian was pursuing/hunting out/attacking my father."

One cannot simply side with modern translations of Deuteronomy 26:5a without presenting clear argumentation for ignoring the masoretic accents.

Example #4: Deuteronomy 32:5a
שִׁחֵת לוֹ לֹא בָּנָיו מוּמָם
Has he acted corruptly toward himself? No!
His children—it's their fault.

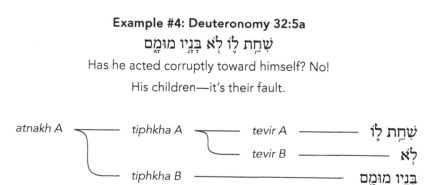

The NIV and ESV agree in reading לֹא בָּנָיו together and translating it as "not his children" and "no longer his children," respectively. While this reading is grammatically possible, it is not the reading provided by the Masoretes. *Atnakh* A is divided in half by *tiphkha* (לוֹ), separating לֹא from בָּנָיו. When the negative adverb לֹא occurs with a disjunctive accent,[21] as is

---

19. See for example Gen 25:20; 28:5; 31:20, 24; 2 Kgs 5:20.
20. Though passive in form, this verb is a deponent and thus active in meaning.
21. See for example Judg 5:13, 2 Sam 24:24, and Jer 42:14 with *yetiv*; 1 Sam 8:19 and 1 Kgs 11:22 with *zaqeph*; and Josh 5:14 with *revia*.

the case in Deuteronomy 32:5a, it typically means "No!" absolutely and does not negate what follows. Understanding God as the subject of the initial verb, שִׁחֵת, avoids the need to render this masculine singular ("he") with a plural ("they"), as in the NIV and the ESV. Since the interrogatory *he* is not necessary for there to be a question,[22] it is not at all a stretch to take שִׁחֵת לֹ֖ו (*tevir* A) as a question: "Has he [God] acted corruptly toward himself?" The answer is then provided: לֹ֖א (*tevir* B). The blame does not fall on God (*tiphkha* A); the blame falls on God's children (*tiphkha* B).

ERRORS

"Even Homer nods," as the saying goes. Or should we say, "Even the Masoretes make mistakes"? In my reading of the secondary literature I have not come across anyone who would say that the masoretic tradition is error free. Not even those who affirm that the vowels and the accents are inspired make that claim.[23] So let's conclude this chapter by looking at a couple of texts in which the masoretic accents seem to be incorrect. I say "seem to be" because, as Yeivin has said,

> The scholars who established the accentuation lived long ago, subject to different pressures from ours, and in a different thought-world. For this reason, it is often difficult to understand the reason for some particular detail of the placing of the accent signs in a verse.[24]

Example #1: Isaiah 40:3a

קֹ֣ול קֹורֵ֔א בַּמִּדְבָּ֕ר

פַּנּ֖ו דֶּ֥רֶךְ יְהֹוָ֑ה

A voice is calling in the wilderness,

"Prepare the way for the LORD."

---

22. *BHRG* §43.2.2.
23. Fuller and Choi, *Hebrew Syntax*, 352.
24. Yeivin, *Introduction to the Tiberian Masorah*, 171.

קוֹל קוֹרֵא ——————————————— atnakh A ⌐ zaqeph A ———————————

בַּמִּדְבָּר ————————— zaqeph B ⌐ zaqeph gadol A ———————

פַּנּוּ —————— zaqeph gadol B ⌐ tiphkha A ————

דֶּרֶךְ יְהֹוָה — tiphkha B

This half verse is divided in half by *zaqeph* (קוֹרֵא), so the masoretic interpretation is,

A voice is calling: (*zaqeph* A)
   In the wilderness prepare the way for the Lord. (*zaqeph* B)

Most modern translations follow this interpretation.[25]

The first thing that catches my eye in the masoretic reading is the imbalance in the cola of this poetic line: 2 words (קוֹל קוֹרֵא) + 4 words (בַּמִּדְבָּר פַּנּוּ דֶּרֶךְ יְהֹוָה). While such a line is certainly possible, reading 3 words (קוֹל קוֹרֵא בַּמִּדְבָּר) + 3 words (פַּנּוּ דֶּרֶךְ יְהֹוָה) provides better balance. A second factor to consider is the opening line in verse 6, which is composed of 3 words + 3 words:

קוֹל אֹמֵר קְרָא וְאָמַר מָה אֶקְרָא
A voice says, "Cry out." And I said, "What shall I cry?"

Then there is the matter of ancient translations. The Septuagint renders this verse with

φωνὴ βοῶντος ἐν τῇ ἐρήμῳ
Ἑτοιμάσατε τὴν ὁδὸν κυρίου
A voice is calling in the desert,
"Prepare the way of the Lord."

And the Latin Vulgate is similar,

---

25. See for example the ESV, NASB, NIV, NLT, NRSV, and NJPS.

Vox clamantis in deserto:
Parate viam Domini
A voice is calling in the desert,
"Prepare the way of the Lord."

Finally, there is the consideration of the New Testament quotation of this verse in Matthew 3:3.[26]

φωνὴ βοῶντος ἐν τῇ ἐρήμῳ
ἑτοιμάσατε τὴν ὁδὸν κυρίου
"A voice of one calling in the wilderness,
'Prepare the way for the Lord. . . .'"

The masoretic reading of Isaiah 40:3a is clearly out of sync with other streams in ancient tradition,[27] and it seems to be so erroneously.

Example #2: Numbers 13:33a

וְשָׁם רָאִינוּ אֶת־הַנְּפִילִים בְּנֵי עֲנָק מִן־הַנְּפִלִים

There we saw the Nephilim; the sons of Anak are from the Nephilim.

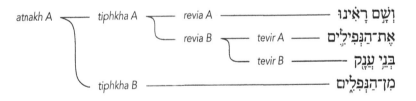

This half verse is divided in half by *tiphkha* (עֲנָק). Given the rule of daughter associations that we have seen earlier, *tiphkha* B (מִן־הַנְּפִלִים) should qualify the whole of *tiphkha* A (וְשָׁם רָאִינוּ אֶת־הַנְּפִילִים בְּנֵי עֲנָק), but it is difficult if not impossible to see how this makes any sense.

The obvious sense of the text is that בְּנֵי עֲנָק מִן־הַנְּפִלִים provides additional information with regard to הַנְּפִילִים. The NIV and the ESV show

---

26. See also Mark 1:3.
27. For a brief discussion of how 1QS 8.13–14 (כאשר כתוב במדבר פנו דרך, "As it is written, 'In the wilderness prepare a way'") supports the masoretic accents; see Khan, *A Short Introduction*, 40.

a correct sensitivity by taking בְּנֵי עֲנָק מִן־הַנְּפִלִים as parenthetical, and if they are correct, the masoretic accents are incorrect, because if a parenthesis starts after אֶת־הַנְּפִילִים (*tevir*), the parenthesis should end at the next accent up the hierarchy, which is *tiphkha* (עֲנָק), and not at *atnakh* (מִן־הַנְּפִלִים).

In terms of sense, this half verse should be divided at אֶת־הַנְּפִילִים, with the main predication being וְשָׁם רָאִינוּ אֶת־הַנְּפִלִים ("There we saw the Nephilim"). The second qualifying predication would then be בְּנֵי עֲנָק מִן־הַנְּפִלִים ("the sons of Anak are from the Nephilim"). So, at minimum we can say that the masoretic accents do not correctly divide the text according to sense.[28]

Example #3: Proverbs 31:1

דִּבְרֵי לְמוּאֵל מֶלֶךְ מַשָּׂא

אֲשֶׁר־יִסְּרַתּוּ אִמּוֹ׃

The words of Lemuel, king of Massa,

with which his mother admonished him: (NJPS)[29]

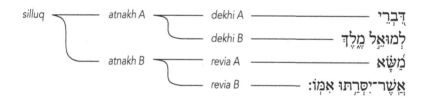

This verse is divided in half at *atnakh* (מֶלֶךְ), so the common translation of this verse separates מֶלֶךְ ("king") from מַשָּׂא ("oracle"). This interpretation of the text, found in most English translations, was already established by the time of the Vulgate:

Verba Lamuelis regis.

Visio qua erudivit eum mater sua.

The words of King Lemuel.

A vision which his mother taught him.

---

28. This may be a case where the musical function of the accents is overriding the syntactic sense of the text. See Wickes, *A Treatise on the Twenty-One*, 3.

29. So too *AFPMA*.

But let's consider a couple of grammatical points.

First, this would be the only verse where מֶ֫לֶךְ would be used in apposition to a personal name but would not be followed by a reference to the country where the king reigned. First Kings 12:23 shows the typical sequence of personal name + מֶ֫לֶךְ + place name.

$$\text{אֱמֹר אֶל־רְחַבְעָם בֶּן־שְׁלֹמֹה מֶ֫לֶךְ יְהוּדָה}$$
Say to Rehoboam son of Solomon king of Judah

Examples could be multiplied, but one is most salient because it occurs in the book of Proverbs, and it occurs in the exact same context as Proverbs 31:1, that is, in a title to a collection of proverbs. In Proverbs 1:1 we read,

$$\text{מִשְׁלֵי שְׁלֹמֹה בֶן־דָּוִד מֶ֫לֶךְ יִשְׂרָאֵל׃}$$
The proverbs of Solomon, son of David, king of Israel:

A related example from the wisdom literature is Ecclesiastes 1:1.

$$\text{דִּבְרֵי קֹהֶלֶת בֶּן־דָּוִד מֶ֫לֶךְ בִּירוּשָׁלָ֑͏ִם׃}$$
The words of the teacher, son of David, king in Jerusalem:

These examples lead us to expect that the noun מֶ֫לֶךְ should be followed by a place name, which it is not in Proverbs 31:1.

Second, if the text wanted to say "King Lemuel," we would expect it to say הַמֶּ֫לֶךְ לְמוּאֵל, as in 1 Kings 4:1.

$$\text{וַיְהִי הַמֶּ֫לֶךְ שְׁלֹמֹה מֶ֫לֶךְ עַל־כָּל־יִשְׂרָאֵל׃}$$
King Solomon was king over all Israel.

So, it seems that the Hebrew underlying "the words of King Lemuel" should be דִּבְרֵי לְמוּאֵל הַמֶּ֫לֶךְ.

Given the above, especially the expectation of a place name after the sequence of a personal name + מֶ֫לֶךְ, as we saw in 1 Kings 12:23, a simple solution is to understand מַשָּׂא as III מַשָּׂא ("Massa")[30] instead of II מַשָּׂא ("oracle"), as proposed in *DCH*[31] and adopted in the NJPS.[32] The verse would then be divided in half at מַשָּׂא and the accents would be:

דִּבְרֵי לְמוּאֵל מֶלֶךְ מַשָּׂא אֲשֶׁר־יִסְּרַתּוּ אִמּוֹ:

The words of Lemuel, king of Massa, with which
his mother admonished him: (NJPS)

I must admit that it feels rather presumptuous for me to be correcting the venerable tradition of the Masoretes. But as I said at the beginning of this section, "even Homer nods."

30. Massa was an area in North Arabia.
31. *DCH* 5.498, "or em. מֶלֶךְ מַשָּׂא the words of Lemuel, a king; a pronouncement that his mother taught him, to מֶלֶךְ מַשָּׂא the words of Lemuel, king of Massa, whose mother taught him."
32. So too *AFPMA*.

CHAPTER 5

THE ACCENTS IN
THE THREE

This book is a basic introduction to the masoretic accents and in particular to the accents in what are called the Twenty-One books of the Hebrew Bible. In this chapter you will be introduced to the accents in the Three. The Three include Psalms, the poetical section of Job, and Proverbs. I said in the introduction to the book that the accents are complicated and can be perplexing. If the accents are complicated in the Twenty-One, they are more so in the Three. One scholar has said,

> Hence it is not strange that most scholars have left the decipherment of the accents of the "Three Books" until all other problems of the universe have been solved.[1]

I also said in the introduction that you did not have to become a master of every detail of the accents in the Twenty-One to have a beneficial working knowledge of these accents. The same is true for the accents in the Three.

To provide you with even a basic introduction to the accents in the Three, I would need the same number of pages used to introduce the accents in the Twenty-One. So, this chapter is intended to simply give you an overview of the basics of the accents in the Three. First, we will look at the names and the symbols, and you will find that you are already familiar with many of them. Second, I will provide you with some notes that will help you understand the functions of these accents. Third, we will take a brief look at Psalm 29 to give you some practice in reading the accents in the Three.

---

1. Davis, *The Hebrew Accents of the Twenty-One Books of the Bible*, 14.

NAMES AND SYMBOLS

Group	Hebrew Name	English Name	Symbol	Symbol
Group 1	סִלּוּק	silluq	טטט	◌ֽ
	עוֹלֶה וְיוֹרֵד	ole veyored	טטט	◌ֺ◌֥
	אַתְנָח	atnakh	טטט	◌֑
Group 2	רְבִיעַ גָּדוֹל	revia gadol	טטֹ	◌ֺ
	רְבִיעַ מֻגְרָשׁ	revia mugrash	טטֹ	◌ֺ◌ֺ
	שַׁלְשֶׁלֶת גָּדוֹל	shalshelet gadol	טטֹ׀	׀◌ֺ
	רְבִיעַ קָטוֹן	revia qaton	טטֹ	◌ֺ
	צִנּוֹר	tsinnor	טטֺ	◌ֺ
	דְּחִי	dechi	טטט	◌ֶ
Group 3	פָּזֶר	pazer	טטֹ	◌֥
	מְהֻפָּח לְגַרְמֶהּ	mehuppakh legarmeh	טטט׀	׀◌ֻ
	אַזְלָא לְגַרְמֶהּ	azla legarmeh	טטֺ׀	׀◌ֺ

NOTES

Hebrew Name	English Name	Symbol	Symbol
מוּנַח	munakh	טטט	◌ֻ
מֵרְכָא	merekha	טטט	◌֥
עִלּוּי	illuy	טטֹ	◌ֺ
טַרְחָא	tarkha	טטט	◌֑
גַּלְגַּל	galgal	טטט	◌֦
מְהֻפָּח	mehuppakh	טטט	◌ֻ
אַזְלָא	azla	טטֺ	◌ֺ
שַׁלְשֶׁלֶת קְטַנָּה	shalshelet qetannah	טֹ	◌ֺ
צִנּוֹרִית מֵרְכָא	tsinnorit merekha	טטֺ	◌ֺ◌ֺ
צִנּוֹרִית מְהֻפָּח	tsinnorit mehuppakh	טטֺ	◌ֺ◌ֺ

1. There are fewer disjunctive accents in the Three than in the Twenty-One (twelve, not eighteen), and there are only three hierarchical groups, not four.

2. Comments on some disjunctive accents:

    a. *Ole veyored* ֺֹ is composed of two symbols. The first is *mehuppakh*, but it sits above the word not under the word as in the Twenty-One, and the second is *merekha*. *Ole veyored* usually occurs on a single word, but it can be split over a two-word unit as in עַל־פַּלְגֵי מָיִם ("by streams of water," Ps 1:3).

    b. *Revia mugrash* ֺֹ is composed of two symbols. The second is *revia* and the first is *geresh*, hence the name *revia mugrash*. *Revia mugrash* is the functional equivalent of *tiphkha* in the Twenty-One, as *revia mugrash* is also the final disjunctive accent before *silluq* (with the possibility of an intervening *merekha*).[2]

    c. *Shalshelet gadol* |ֺ (known simply as *shalshelet* in the Twenty-One) is composed of two symbols, *shalshelet* + *paseq*. *Shalshelet gadol* is a substitute for *revia mugrash*.

    d. *Revia qaton* ֺ only occurs before *ole veyored*; any other occurrence of the *revia* symbol will be *revia gadol* ֺ.[3]

    e. *Tsinnor* ֺ is the same symbol as *zarqa* in the Twenty-One, but *tsinnor* is postpositive.

    f. *Dekhi* ֺ is the same symbol as *tiphkha*, but *dekhi* is prepositive. Like *tiphkha*, *dekhi* occurs before *atnakh* (with the possibility of an intervening conjunctive accent).

    g. *Mehuppakh legarmeh* |ֺ and *azla legarmeh* |ֺ are both composed of two symbols, *mehuppakh* + *paseq* and *azla* + *paseq*. Whereas *mehuppakh* and *azla* are conjunctive in the Twenty-One, *mehuppakh legarmeh* and *azla legarmeh* are disjunctive in the Three.

3. The same governing principle of continuous dichotomy is operative in the Three.

4. *Silluq* is the major disjunctive accent that brings every verse to a close.

---

2. Wickes, *A Treatise on the Accentuation of the Three*, 15–16; Fuller and Choi, *Hebrew Syntax*, 365.
3. Wickes, *A Treatise on the Accentuation of the Three*, 12n10.

5. Your first step in reading with the accents remains the same: establish the main dichotomy of the verse. Most of the time the main dichotomy will be marked by *atnakh*, but sometimes it will be marked by *ole veyored*. In general, *atnakh* marks the major dichotomy in shorter verses, while *ole veyored* marks it in longer verses.[4]

6. If *ole veyored* divides a verse in half, *atnakh* may divide the second half of the verse in half.

7. Where the major dichotomy is marked correlates frequently with the parallelism of the poetic line. If the line is a bicolon, the main dichotomy falls on the last word of the first colon.[5] If the line is a tricolon, the main dichotomy tends to keep the two similar cola together. If the tricolon contains three parallel thoughts, the main dichotomy tends to occur at the end of the first colon, since the first colon typically contains the main thought that will be amplified by the following two cola.[6]

8. Having established the main dichotomy, you can then establish the subsequent dichotomies, as you learned to do in the Twenty-One. A unit ending in *silluq*, *ole veyored*, or *atnakh* will frequently be divided in half by one of the three *revias*.

9. Comments on some conjunctive accents:

   a. Some conjunctives you are already familiar with from the Twenty-One do not occur in the Three and a few new ones do. Those that do not occur are *merekha kephulah*, *darga*, and *telisha qetannah*. The new ones are *illuy*, *tarcha*, *shalshelet qetannah*, *tsinnorit merekha*, and *tsinnorit mehuppakh*.

---

4. In particular, if the major dichotomy is one, two, or three words before *silluq*, then *atnakh* is used; if the major dichotomy is four or five words before *silluq*, then either *atnakh* or *ole veyored* is used; if the major dichotomy is six or more words before *silluq*, then *ole veyored* marks the major dichotomy. See Wickes, *A Treatise on the Accentuation of the Three*, 30; Fuller and Choi, *Hebrew Syntax*, 367n22.
5. Wickes, *A Treatise on the Accentuation of the Three*, 27.
6. Wickes, *A Treatise on the Accentuation of the Three*, 28–29; Fuller and Choi, *Hebrew Syntax*, 392.

b. *Illuy* ⊙̇ is the same symbol as *munakh*, but *illuy* is placed above the word not below it.

c. *Tarcha* ⊙̣ is the same symbol as *tiphkha*, but *tiphkha* does not occur in the Three.

d. *Shalshelet qetannah* ⊙̇ is the same symbol as *shalshelet gadol* minus *paseq*.

e. *Tsinnorit* ⊙̈ contains the same symbol as *tsinnor*. Unlike *tsinnor*, which is postpositive, *tsinnorit* is pretonic, that is, it always occurs in an open syllable and always before either *merekha* or *mehuppakh*, which marks the stressed syllable, hence the names *tsinnorit merekha* ⊙̣⊙̈ and *tsinnorit mehuppakh* ⊙̣⊙̈. As with *ole veyored*, *tsinnorit merekha* and *tsinnorit mehuppakh* can occur on a two-word unit, as in אָמַ֣ר אֵלַ֗י ("He said to me," Ps 2:7).[7]

EXAMPLE: PSALM 29

Verse 1

מִזְמ֗וֹר לְדָוִ֥ד

הָב֣וּ לַֽיהוָ֔ה בְּנֵ֖י אֵלִ֑ים

הָב֥וּ לַֽיהוָ֗ה כָּב֥וֹד וָעֹֽז׃

A psalm of David.

Ascribe to the Lᴏʀᴅ, sons of gods,

ascribe to the Lᴏʀᴅ glory and strength.

Ole veyored (לְדָוִ֥ד) divides this verse in half, separating the title from the first line of poetry. *Ole veyored* is used to mark the main dichotomy, since it occurs six or more words from *silluq*. *Atnakh* (אֵלִ֑ים) separates the first colon from the second colon. The first colon answers the question *who*, and the second colon answers the question *what*.

---

7. Wickes, *A Treatise on the Accentuation of the Three*, 22–23.

Verse 2

הָבוּ לַיהוָה כְּבוֹד שְׁמוֹ

הִשְׁתַּחֲווּ לַיהוָה בְּהַדְרַת־קֹדֶשׁ׃

Ascribe to the Lord the glory of his name;

bow down to the Lord in the splendor of his holiness.

Atnakh (שְׁמוֹ) divides this verse in half, separating the first colon from the second colon. *Atnakh* is used to mark the main dichotomy, since the main dichotomy is only three words before *silluq*. The first colon specifies the nature of the "glory" mentioned in the previous colon, and the second colon answers the question *when*.[8]

Verse 3

קוֹל יְהוָה עַל־הַמָּיִם

אֵל־הַכָּבוֹד הִרְעִים

יְהוָה עַל־מַיִם רַבִּים׃

The voice of the Lord is over the waters;

the God of glory thunders,

the Lord thunders over the mighty waters. (NIV)

Ole veyored (עַל־הַמָּיִם) divides this verse in half. *Ole veyored* is used to mark the main dichotomy. When the main dichotomy is four or five words from *silluq*, either *ole veyored* or *atnakh* can mark this main division, but at five words, as is the case, here the tendency is to use *ole veyored*. *Atnakh* (הִרְעִים) then divides the second half of the verse in half. Note how the NIV captures these divisions by placing a semicolon after the first colon and a comma after the second colon. The first colon contains the main idea: the thunderstorm is brewing over "the waters," that is, the Mediterranean. The second two cola amplify this by specifying that the thunder is not just any thunder but it is the thunder of "the God of glory," and that "the waters" are

---

8. "This phrase is often understood as referring to the appearance of the worshipers—their appropriate attire or attitude . . . But it is better understood as a reference to the appearance of the Lord in the splendor of the storm described in 29:3–9 . . . ." Mark D. Futato, *Psalms*, vol. 7 of *Cornerstone Biblical Commentary* (Downers Grove, IL: Tyndale House Publishers, 2009), 119.

not just any waters but "the mighty waters," an allusion to the waters that stand in opposition to God's well-ordered creation.[9]

Verse 4

קוֹל־יְהוָה בַּכֹּחַ
קוֹל יְהוָה בֶּהָדָר׃

The voice of the Lord in power;
the voice of the Lord in majesty.

Atnakh (בַּכֹּחַ) divides this verse in half, separating the first colon from the second colon. *Atnakh* is used to mark the main dichotomy, since the main dichotomy is only three words before *silluq*. Verse 1b issues a call to ascribe "strength/power" and "glory" to the Lord. These two cola in verse 4 answer this call.

Verse 5

קוֹל יְהוָה שֹׁבֵר אֲרָזִים
וַיְשַׁבֵּר יְהוָה אֶת־אַרְזֵי הַלְּבָנוֹן׃

The voice of the Lord breaks the cedars;
the Lord shatters the cedars of Lebanon.

Atnakh (אֲרָזִים) divides this verse in half, separating the first colon from the second colon. When the main dichotomy is four or five words from *silluq*, either *ole veyored* or *atnakh* can mark this main division, but at four words, as is the case here, the tendency is to use *atnakh*. The first colon describes the power of the storm via its ability to break cedars in general, and the next colon amplifies this by referring to them as "the cedars of Lebanon." This would be like referring to redwood trees and then referring to California redwood trees, which are known for their great size.

---

9. See Ps 93:4; see also Isa 17:13; Hab 3:5; Ps 32:6.

Verse 6

וַיַּרְקִידֵם כְּמוֹ־עֵגֶל
לְבָנוֹן וְשִׂרְיֹן כְּמוֹ בֶן־רְאֵמִים:

He makes them leap like a calf,
Lebanon and Sirion like a young wild ox.

Atnakh (כְּמוֹ־עֵגֶל) divides this verse in half, separating the first colon from the second colon. *Atnakh* is used to mark the main dichotomy, since the main dichotomy is four words before *silluq*. The suffix on וַיַּרְקִידֵם is frequently interpreted as an enclitic *mem*, a particle of uncertain function.[10] Modern translations (ESV, NIV, NLT, and RSV) follow this interpretation of the *mem*, ignore the accents, and divide the verse after לְבָנוֹן. In chapter 4 we looked at texts where the masoretic accents seem to be wrong, but there is no need to go against the accents when a suitable interpretation is at hand. The suffix could just as easily be the third-person masculine plural object suffix,[11] used to anticipate the plural direct object, "Sirion and Lebanon." The KJV captures this sense that accords with the masoretic accents, "He maketh them also to skip like a calf; Lebanon and Sirion like a young unicorn.

Verse 7

קוֹל־יְהוָה חֹצֵב
לַהֲבוֹת אֵשׁ:

The voice of the Lord strikes
with flashes of lightning.

Revia qaton (חֹצֵב) divides this very short verse in half, separating the subject and predicate from the adverbial accusative.

---

10. WO §9.8.
11. *BHRG* §17.3.2.3.

Verse 8

קוֹל יְהוָה יָחִיל מִדְבָּר
יָחִיל יְהוָה מִדְבַּר קָדֵשׁ:

The voice of the LORD shakes the desert;
the LORD shakes the desert of Kadesh.

Atnakh (כְּמוֹ־עֵגֶל) divides this verse in half, separating the first colon from the second colon. *Atnakh* is used to mark the main dichotomy, since the main dichotomy is four words before *silluq*. The first colon identifies the last geographical location to experience the storm in general, "the desert," and the second colon provides greater specificity, "the desert of Kadesh," no doubt located somewhere to the east of Mount Hermon.

Verse 9

קוֹל יְהוָה| יְחוֹלֵל אַיָּלוֹת
וַיֶּחֱשֹׂף יְעָרוֹת
וּבְהֵיכָלוֹ כֻּלּוֹ אֹמֵר כָּבוֹד:

The voice of the LORD twists the oaks
and strips the forests bare.
And in his temple all cry, "There is the glory!"

Ole veyored (יְעָרוֹת) divides this verse in half, separating the two similar cola from the dissimilar colon: twisting the oaks (reading אַיָּלוֹת as אֵלִים) and stripping the forest are more closely related to each other than to the cry "There is the glory!" in the (heavenly)[12] temple. Since the major dichotomy occurs four words before *silluq*, either *ole veyored* or *atnakh* could be used to mark the division. *Tsinnor* (אַיָּלוֹת) divides the first half of the verse in half, separating the first two cola. *Atnakh* (וּבְהֵיכָלוֹ) divides the second half of the verse in half, separating the prepositional phrase of location from the subject and predicate.

---

12. "In the context of 29:1–2 the 'temple' is the heavenly temple where the angelic host has always shouted, 'There is the glory!' when the Lord's glory and power appeared in the first storms of the fall . . . The angelic host is called upon in 29:1–2 to follow suit when the Lord's glory appears in the coming fall storms. Implicit is the call to worshipers in the earthly Temple to join the chorus." Futato, *Psalms*, 120.

Verse 10

יְהֹוָה לַמַּבּוּל יָשָׁב

וַיֵּשֶׁב יְהֹוָה מֶלֶךְ לְעוֹלָם׃

The Lord has taken his throne over the flood;

the Lord has taken his throne as king forever.

Atnakh (יָשָׁב) divides this verse in half, separating the first colon from the second colon. *Atnakh* is used to mark the main dichotomy, since the main dichotomy is four words before *silluq*; at four words, *ole veyored* could have been used, as was the case in verse 9, but the tendency in this case is to use *atnakh*. The first colon describes the Lord as having taken his throne over the threatening "mighty waters," referred to in verse 3b, and the second colon adds to this by asserting that the Lord has taken his throne as king forever.

Verse 11

יְהֹוָה עֹז לְעַמּוֹ יִתֵּן

יְהֹוָה ׀ יְבָרֵךְ אֶת־עַמּוֹ בַשָּׁלוֹם׃

The Lord will give strength to his people;

the Lord will bless his people with peace.

Atnakh (יִתֵּן) divides this verse in half, separating the first colon from the second colon. *Atnakh* is used to mark the main dichotomy, since the main dichotomy is four words before *silluq*; at four words, *ole veyored* could have been used, as was the case in verse 9, but the tendency in this case is to use *atnakh*. The results of the coming of this powerful thunderstorm described in verses 3–9 are not destructive for the Lord's people but are beneficial, as they provide everything that the Lord's people need for strength in every area of life (v. 11a) and for overall prosperity (v. 11b).

APPENDIX 1

DETERMINING THE ACCENTS IN A VERSE

Most introductory Hebrew grammars have as their goal teaching students to read Hebrew texts but not to compose Hebrew texts. In the same way, this book has as its goal teaching students to read Hebrew texts with the accents but not to compose accented Hebrew texts. Even the major treatment of the Hebrew accents by Yeivin has a similar modest goal: "However our intention is to understand the accentuation as it is, and not to speculate on the reasons for the use of the accents in individual verses."[1] Yeivin does, however, go on to provide "a preliminary guide to the division of simple phrases and short verses."[2] In this appendix, I am providing you with a concise summary of Yeivin's preliminary guide. I have reduced Yeivin's guide to four points, and I supplemented it with one final point.

Point #1

In general, the main division is placed near the midpoint of the text, midpoint in terms of syntax or semantics and not word count. So, for example, a verse containing two clauses will typically have the main division at the end of the first clause.

Genesis 1:4

וַיַּ֤רְא אֱלֹהִים֙ אֶת־הָא֖וֹר כִּי־ט֑וֹב
וַיַּבְדֵּ֣ל אֱלֹהִ֔ים בֵּ֥ין הָא֖וֹר וּבֵ֥ין הַחֹֽשֶׁךְ׃

God saw that the light was good,
and he separated the light from the darkness.

---

1. Yeivin, *Introduction to the Tiberian Masorah*, 172.
2. Yeivin, *Introduction to the Tiberian Masorah*, 175.

The two clauses are separated by *atnakh* (כִּי־טֽוֹב).

Introductory material, such as the introduction to speech, is usually incorporated into the first half of the verse and does not itself constitute that first half. So, in Genesis 1:3 the major division separates the two clauses of the speech and includes the introduction to the speech in the first half of the verse.

Genesis 1:3

וַיֹּאמֶר אֱלֹהִים יְהִי אֹור
וַֽיְהִי־אֹֽור׃

And God said, "Let there be light,"
and there was light.

The two clauses are separated by *atnakh* (אֹֽור). And the clause that introduces the speech is separated from the speech by *tiphkha* (אֱלֹהִים).

Point #2

Subjects and predicates or words with similar grammatical relationships are typically connected by a conjunctive accent.

Genesis 1:1

בָּרָ֣א אֱלֹהִ֑ים
God created

The predicate is joined to the subject by *munakh* (בָּרָ֣א).

Point #3

Words in a construct chain are typically connected by a conjunctive accent.

Genesis 1:14

בִּרְקִ֣יעַ הַשָּׁמַ֑יִם
the vault of the sky

The preposition and first noun of the construct chain are joined to the second noun of the chain by *munakh* (בִּרְקִיעַ).

Point #4

Small words followed by a word with a disjunctive accent typically have either a conjunctive accent or *maqqeph*.

Genesis 1:1

אֵת הַשָּׁמַיִם

the heavens

The definite direct object marker is joined to the direct object by *merekha* (אֵת).

Genesis 1:4

כִּי־טוֹב

that it was good

The conjunction (כִּי) is joined to the following word by *maqqeph*.

Point #5

Yeivin's preliminary guide can be supplemented with a paragraph from Fuller and Choi:

> The accents group words into units as a rule, a clause of two words is grouped together with the conjunctive accent; a clause of three words, by contrast, introduces a disjunctive accent within the unit. The same is true of a word or phrase units; a word or phrase unit of two words groups the words with a conjunctive accent; a word or phrase unit of three words introduces a disjunctive accent within the unit.[3]

Here are a few examples.

---

3. Fuller and Choi, *Hebrew Syntax*, 353.

Genesis 1:3

וַיֹּאמֶר אֱלֹהִים

And God said

The predicate of the clause is joined to the subject by the conjunctive *merekha* (וַיֹּאמֶר).

Genesis 1:4

וַיַּרְא אֱלֹהִים אֶת־הָאוֹר

And God saw the light

The subject and the predicate are joined by the conjunctive *darga* (וַיַּרְא), according to Yeivin's point 2, and separated from the direct object by the disjunctive *tevir* (אֱלֹהִים).

Genesis 1:4

בֵּין הָאוֹר

between the light

The preposition is joined to the noun that it governs by the conjunctive *merekha* (בֵּין).

Genesis 1:11

עֵשֶׂב מַזְרִיעַ זֶרַע

vegetation producing seed

The first noun in the construct chain is separated from the second two nouns by the disjunctive *yetiv* (עֵשֶׂב), and the second two nouns are joined by the conjunctive *munakh* (מַזְרִיעַ).

APPENDIX 2

FOR FURTHER STUDY

Some students will not go beyond their knowledge of Hebrew grammar gained through their basic introduction to Hebrew. If they do not, I contend that they will be better interpreters of their Old Testament if they rightly use the modicum of Hebrew grammar that they have learned. But other students will want to acquire advanced knowledge through the study of Hebrew reference grammars. In the same way, some readers of this book will not go beyond the knowledge they have attained from this study. If they do not, I contend that they will be better interpreters of their Hebrew Bible through the modicum of knowledge they have gained. Yet some students will want to advance their knowledge of the Hebrew accents, so this appendix offers a few suggestions.

First, a good next step would be to study the section on the accents found in this resource:

- Fuller, Russell T., and Kyoungwon Choi. *Invitation to Biblical Hebrew Syntax: An Intermediate Grammar*. Grand Rapids: Kregel Academic, 2017.

A good way to practice reading with the accents is to carefully work through the examples analyzed on pages 372–413.[1]

Second, for a more detailed study of the linguistic approach used in this book, read the following resources:

---

1. There will be a bit of a learning curve, since Fuller and Choi use the descriptive system of "Emperors," "Kings," etc.

- Barrick, William D. "The Masoretic Hebrew Accents in Translation and Interpretation," n.d. http://drbarrick.org/files/papers/other/HebrewAccentsrev.pdf.
- Robinson, David, and Elisabeth Levy. "Masoretic Hebrew Cantillation and Constituent Structure Analysis." *British & Foreign Bible Society*, May 2, 2002. http://lc.bfbs.org.uk/e107_files/downloads/masoretes.pdf.
- ———. "The Masoretes and the Punctuation of Biblical Hebrew." *British & Foreign Bible Society*, May 2, 2002. http://lc.bfbs.org.uk/e107_files/downloads/masoretes.pdf.

The article by Barrick is basic and brief, so it is a good introduction. The two articles by Robinson and Levi are more sophisticated, and you will benefit greatly from studying them.

Third, though the following books are older and at times use outdated language, you will do well to study them:

- Davis, Arthur. *The Hebrew Accents of the Twenty-One Books of the Bible*. Repr., Leopold Classic Library, 1900.
- Wickes, William. *A Treatise on the Accentuation of the Three So-Called Poetical Books on the Old Testament, Psalms, Proverbs, and Job*. Repr., Oxford: Clarendon, 1881.
- ———. *A Treatise on the Accentuation of the Twenty-One So-Called Prose Books of the Old Testament: With a Facsimile of a Page of the Codex Assigned to Ben-Asher in Aleppo*. Repr., Oxford: Clarendon, 1887.

Fourth, the best two reference works to have at your disposal are these:

- Price, James D. *Concordance of the Hebrew Accents in the Hebrew Bible*. 5 vols. New York: Mellen, 1996.
- Yeivin, Israel. *Introduction to the Tiberian Masorah*. Translated by E. J. Revell. The Society of Biblical Literature Masoretic Studies 5. Missoula, MT: Scholars Press, 1980.

The former is a monumental work that provides a concordance of the accents as they are used in each of the divisions of the Hebrew canon. In addition to the concording of the accents, this work contains excellent brief descriptions of the use of the various accents in relation to the other accents. [Note: accent sensitive searching can be executed in Accordance, BibleWorks, and Logos.] The latter is a classic treatment of the Masoretic Text with an extensive section on the accents.

Of course, there is no substitute for picking up these tools and reading, reading, reading your Hebrew Bible slowly, verse by verse, paying attention to the sense of the text encoded in the masoretic accents.

BIBLIOGRAPHY OF WORKS CITED

Barrick, William D. "The Masoretic Hebrew Accents in Translation and Interpretation," n.d. http://drbarrick.org/files/papers/other/HebrewAccentsrev.pdf.

Berlin, Adele, Marc Zvi Brettler, and Michael A. Fishbane, eds. *The Jewish Study Bible: Jewish Publication Society Tanakh Translation*. Oxford: Oxford University Press, 2004.

Davis, Arthur. *The Hebrew Accents of the Twenty-One Books of the Bible*. Repr., Leopold Classic Library, 1900.

Fuller, Russell T., and Kyoungwon Choi. *Invitation to Biblical Hebrew Syntax: An Intermediate Grammar*. Grand Rapids: Kregel Academic, 2017.

Futato, Mark D. *Beginning Biblical Hebrew*. Winona Lake, IN: Eisenbrauns, 2003.

———. *Psalms. Cornerstone Biblical Commentary 7*. Downers Grove, IL: Tyndale House Publishers, 2009.

Garrett, Duane A., and Jason S. DeRouchie. *A Modern Grammar for Biblical Hebrew*. Nashville: Broadman & Holman, 2009.

Joüon, Paul, and T. Muraoka. *A Grammar of Biblical Hebrew*. 2nd ed. Roma: Gregorian & Biblical Press, 2011.

Khan, Geoffrey. *A Short Introduction to the Tiberian Masoretic Bible and Its Reading Tradition*. 2nd ed. Piscataway, NJ: Gorgias, 2014.

Lambdin, Thomas O. *Introduction to Biblical Hebrew*. London: Darton, Longman, & Todd, 1973.

Lehman, Marcus A. *Reading with the Masoretes: The Exegetical Utility of Masoretic Accent Patterns*. Wilmore, KY: GlossaHouse, 2019.

Merwe, Christo H. J. van der, J. A. Naudé, and J. H. Kroeze. *A Biblical Hebrew Reference Grammar*. 2nd ed. London: T&T Clark, 2017.

Pratico, Gary D., and Miles V. van Pelt. *Basics of Biblical Hebrew Grammar*. 2nd ed. Zondervan, 2014.

Price, James D. *Concordance of the Hebrew Accents in the Hebrew Bible*. 5 vols. New York: Mellen, 1996.

———. *The Syntax of Masoretic Accents in the Hebrew Bible: Studies in the Bible and Early Christianity*. New York: Mellen, 1990.

Robinson, David, and Elisabeth Levy. "Masoretic Hebrew Cantillation and Constituent Structure Analysis." *British & Foreign Bible Society*, May 2, 2002. http://lc.bfbs.org.uk/e107_files/downloads/masoretes.pdf.

———. "The Masoretes and the Punctuation of Biblical Hebrew." *British & Foreign Bible Society*, May 2, 2002. http://lc.bfbs.org.uk/e107_files /downloads/masoretes.pdf.

Walker-Jones, Arthur. *Hebrew for Biblical Interpretation*. Atlanta: Society of Biblical Literature, 2003.

Waltke, Bruce K., and M. O'Connor. *An Introduction to Biblical Hebrew Syntax*. Winona Lake, IN: Eisenbrauns, 1990.

Wickes, William. *A Treatise on the Accentuation of the Three So-Called Poetical Books on the Old Testament, Psalms, Proverbs, and Job*. Repr., Oxford: Clarendon, 1881.

———. *A Treatise on the Accentuation of the Twenty-One So-Called Prose Books of the Old Testament: With a Facsimile of a Page of the Codex Assigned to Ben-Asher in Aleppo*. Repr., Oxford: Clarendon, 1887.

Yeivin, Israel. *Introduction to the Tiberian Masorah*. Translated by E. J. Revell. The Society of Biblical Literature Masoretic Studies 5. Missoula, MT: Scholars Press, 1980.

SCRIPTURE INDEX

Basics of Biblical Hebrew, Third Edition

Gary D. Pratico, Miles V. Van Pelt

The third edition of *Basics of Biblical Hebrew Grammar* represents a significant updating and revision of the previous edition with the goal of providing students with the best possible tool for learning Biblical Hebrew.
The *Basics of Biblical Hebrew Grammar*:

- Combines the best of inductive and deductive approaches
- Uses actual examples from the Hebrew Old Testament rather than "made-up" illustrations
- Emphasizes the structural pattern of the Hebrew language rather than rote memorization, resulting in a simple, enjoyable, and effective learning process
- Employs colored text that highlights key features of nouns and verbs, allowing easy recognition of new forms
- Includes appendices of verbal paradigms and diagnostics for fast reference and a complete vocabulary glossary
- Displays larger font and text size, making reading easier

By the time students have worked their way through this text they will know:

- The Hebrew Alphabet
- Vocabulary for words occurring 70 times or more in the Hebrew Bible
- The Hebrew noun system
- The Hebrew verbal system

Available in stores and online!

Biblical Hebrew Vocabulary by Conceptual Categories

A Student's Guide to Nouns in the Old Testament

J. David Pleins,
with Jonathan Homrighausen

Biblical Hebrew Vocabulary by Conceptual Categories is an innovative study reference intended for both introductory and advanced students of the Hebrew language to help them understand and remember vocabulary based on logical categories of related words. Since our minds acquire and recall language by making associations between related words it is only natural that we would study language in this way. By organizing Hebrew vocabulary into logical categories, as opposed to frequency, students can quickly begin to familiarize themselves with entire groups of terms and more readily acquaint themselves with the ranges of meaning of particular Hebrew words.

    Biblical Hebrew Vocabulary by Conceptual Categories is intended to move students beyond rote memorization to a more dynamic grasp of Hebrew vocabulary, ultimately equipping them to read with more fluidity and with a deeper and more intuitive grasp of the biblical text.

Available in stores and online!

Biblical Hebrew Vocabulary in Context

Building Competency with Words
Occurring 50 Times of More

Miles V. Van Pelt, Gary D. Pratico

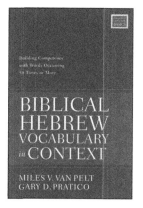

Biblical Hebrew Vocabulary in Context is a biblical Hebrew language resource designed to reinforce a student's basic vocabulary by reading words that occur fifty times or more in the context of the Hebrew Bible.

All 642 of these Hebrew words have been collated into 195 key biblical verses and/or verse fragments to help students practice and retain their Hebrew vocabulary. In lieu of rote memorization, *Biblical Hebrew Vocabulary in Context* reinforces essential vocabulary by reading words in the context of the Hebrew Bible.

Available in stores and online!

ZONDERVAN®
.com

Basics of Hebrew Discourse

A Guide to Working with Hebrew
Prose and Poetry

*Matthew H. Patton, Frederic Clarke
Putnam*

Edited by Miles V. Van Pelt

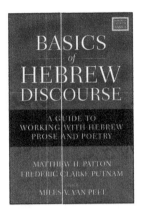

Basics of Hebrew Discourse: A Guide to Working with Hebrew Prose and Poetry by Matthew H. Patton, Frederic Clarke Putnam, and Miles V. Van Pelt is a syntax resource for intermediate Hebrew students. This Basics book introduces students to the principles and exegetical benefits of discourse analysis (text linguistics) when applied to biblical Hebrew prose and poetry. Where standard Hebrew reference grammars have traditionally worked to describe the relationship between words and phrases *within* discrete clauses (micro syntax), discourse analysis works to describe those relationships that exist *between* clauses and texts (macro syntax).

This resource fills a needed gap for intermediate Hebrew students and gives them the tools to work with Hebrew syntax on the macro level. Professors and pastors working with Hebrew will also find this one-of-a-kind resource highly valuable.

The Vocabulary Guide to Biblical Hebrew and Aramaic, Second Edition

Gary D. Pratico, Miles V. Van Pelt

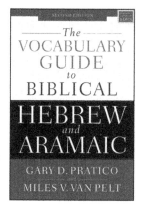

The Vocabulary Guide to Biblical Hebrew and Aramaic, Second Edition by Gary D. Pratico and Miles V. Van Pelt is intended to accompany *Basics of Biblical Hebrew Grammar, Third Edition*. For the beginning student it is an essential resource companion to aid in vocabulary memorization and acquisition. Updates in this second edition include the addition of a complete Aramaic word list and refinement of definitions.

Features include:

- Hebrew words occurring ten times or more in the Old Testament arranged by frequency
- Hebrew words arranged by common root
- All Aramaic words occurring in the Old Testament arranged by frequency
- Helpful appendices including lists of Hebrew homonyms, nominals, and verbs.

Available in stores and online!

Advances in the Study of Biblical Hebrew and Aramaic

Benjamin J. Noonan

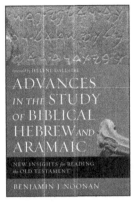

Advances in the Study of Biblical Hebrew and Aramaic by Benjamin J. Noonan is an introduction to issues of interest in the current world of biblical Hebrew and Aramaic scholarship. A growing knowledge of the Semitic languages and the field of linguistics continues to enhance understanding of biblical Hebrew and Aramaic. Comprehension of these items directly affects the way we read the Hebrew Bible and is therefore invaluable for those interested in the Old Testament. This book fills a gap in the field of biblical Hebrew and Aramaic linguistics and provides an accessible, comprehensive, up-to-date, and linguistically informed investigation of the language.

Topics addressed include:

- Linguistic theories
- Lexical semantics and lexicography
- Verbal stems
- Tense, mood, and aspect in the verbal system
- Register, dialect, and code-switching
- Dating of biblical Hebrew and Aramaic texts
- Discourse analysis
- Teaching and learning biblical Hebrew and Aramaic

Advances in the Study of Biblical Hebrew and Aramaic provides an accessible introduction for students, pastors, professors, and commentators to understand these important issues.

Available in stores and online!

Devotions on the Hebrew Bible

54 Reflections to Inspire and Instruct

Milton Eng, Lee M. Fields

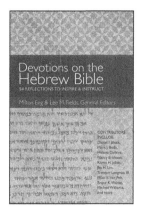

The main point of each devotion in *Devotions on the Hebrew Bible* comes from a careful reading of the passage in the Hebrew Bible, not from an English translation—written by some of the top biblical language scholars of today. Contributors include Daniel I. Block, Mark J. Boda, Hélène Dallaire, Nancy Erickson, Karen H. Jobes, Bo H. Lim, Tremper Longman III, Miles V. Van Pelt, Bruce K. Waltke, and Michael Williams, among others. The authors use a variety of exegetical approaches in their devotions—including grammatical, lexical, rhetorical, sociohistorical, and linguistic—and each devotion closes with a practical application or spiritual reflection.

    Devotions on the Hebrew Bible contains a devotion on every book in the Old Testament and can be used as a weekly devotional or as a supplemental resource throughout a semester or sequence of courses. These devotions will inspire you to keep reading and meditating on the Hebrew Scriptures and find new treasures from the biblical text.

Available in stores and online!

ZONDERVAN®
.com

Dictionary of English Grammar for Students of Biblical Languages

Kyle Greenwood

This succinct and accessible resource will help students of biblical languages gain a better appreciation and understanding of the rules, functions, and terminology of English grammar. Useful for beginners, intermediate, and advanced students this quick reference guide can be used in both biblical languages courses as well as in exegetical courses and as a resource in writing exegetical papers. Instructors will also benefit from the book as both a refresher in grammatical terms and as an additional resource for helping students define terms.

This handy resource provides:

- Definitions of nearly 100 grammatical terms based on their English usage
- Explanations of how terms are used in Greek and Hebrew
- An easy-to-use quick reference tool for beginner, intermediate, and advanced biblical language students
- A useful aid to exegesis
- Alphabetical organization

Available in stores and online!

ZONDERVAN®
.com

Basics of Greek Accents

John A. L. Lee

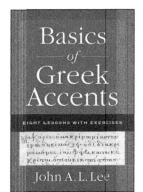

Basics of Greek Accents by John A. L. Lee is a compact, student-friendly, and practical guide to accents for students of both classical and biblical Greek. In eight simple lessons students will learn the basics of ancient Greek accentuation.

Ideal for beginners who are just learning the language or for intermediate students who have learned some Greek but are unsure of their accents, this handy resource avoids theory and concentrates on taking the learner through the essentials in a natural sequence and reinforces learning by means of simple exercises.